The Rwandan Tutsis:
A Tutsi Woman's Account of the Hidden Causes of the Rwandan Tragedy

Published by
Adonis & Abbey Publishers Ltd
P.O. Box 43418
London
SE11 4XZ
http://www.adonis-abbey.com

First Edition, June 2006

Copyright 2006 © Eugenie Mujawiyera

British Library Cataloguing-in-Publication Data
A catalogue record for this book is available from the British Library

ISBN 1-905068-38-7

Cover Design   Mega Graphix

Printed and bound in Great Britain

The Rwandan Tutsis:
A Tutsi Woman's Account of the Hidden Causes of the Rwandan Tragedy

By

Eugenie Mujawiyera

Editorial assistance: Mark H. Teeter

Adonis & Abbey
Publishers Ltd

Contents

Dedication

To the memory of my father, who awakened my spirit and gave me an eternal example of perseverance.

Introduction

Why This Book Was Written

Graduating a few years ago from university with a diploma in literature, I decided not to start publishing my own writings straight away. The reason was simple: a six-year marathon swim through a sea of library books makes you feel as if every subject has already been described by whole flotillas of writers, all of whom claim to know the truth. You even feel that adding more to these books is somehow unfair towards future generations of students. So for the time being, I found a job as a human resources officer in a big company and developed my writing skills mainly by composing corporate reports. I liked the job because it put me in touch with real people, their lives and their problems. I was prepared to dedicate my life to this kind of work. But destiny had another plan for me, sending me a world away from my African homeland to the opposite side of the globe — to Europe. There I had ample opportunity to read peacefully and at my leisure; even more important, I had opportunities to observe and to reflect. And the longer and further I was away from my country, the clearer it became: the world had not run out of important questions — questions which no one, despite the ever-expanding sea of written books, had yet answered.

One of these questions has had a direct effect on me ever since my childhood. I am Rwandan; but I was born in exile and saw my ancestral homeland for the first time only as a grown-up. Before my birth, my parents had been obliged to leave Rwanda and go to the Congo because our family was Tutsi; in those days it was life-threatening for a Tutsi to remain in the country of his ancestors. These were the mid-1960's, just years after the greatest chapter in the struggle of African nations for freedom from colonial enslavement. Paradoxically (for the

Western reader, at least), this era of new freedom also occasioned an era of tragedy, of the greatest bloodletting in the whole of African history. Rwanda is only one stark example of what has happened with millions of Africans—and continues to happen to this day.

No one could ever explain me when I was a child what was so special, so peculiar about my family, my relatives and all the rest of the Tutsi ethnicity, a black-skinned people who seemed to me like any other. By that time no less than half the Rwandan Tutsis lived outside their country, with no right of return, like the ancient Jews. I simply assumed that to be a Tutsi was a kind of a "life-threatening privilege", because wherever we went among different African lands, we had to preserve ourselves by becoming something else—we had to mix with local kids and speak their mother tongue; calling ourselves Tutsi was taboo. The official government of Rwanda denied our Rwandan nationality and wanted us to become assimilated in exile. But none of us had forgotten who we were. Our parents kept their long-outdated Rwandan identity cards.

For centuries, an aura of mystery surrounded the Tutsis. They lived on the large territories of eastern Africa, and in Rwanda their history was particularly glorious. The Tutsis ruled a mighty state there when Christopher Columbus was still preparing to depart for America. Their mountainous kingdom was never in slavery to others. And the first European colonialists—who behaved as they liked upon settling in other countries—could only politely ask the Tutsi king for permission to raise the German flag in the Rwandan hills. In more recent times, after the Tutsis became dispersed across different African countries, many nations acknowledged the dignity and the exceptional moral force of these refugees. Yet these very qualities also gave rise to speculation about secret designs for Tutsi hegemony in east Africa.

To us, exiled Tutsis living for decades with no rights and no nationality, such speculation sounded like a cruel joke. We were barely eking out an existence, allowed to live but required to act as if we were not there. One day the whole of humanity finally came to hear of us—but the price we paid for this recognition was terrible indeed. One of the greatest organized slaughters of innocent civilians in history broke out in front of the entire civilized world. One million people perished, nearly all of them Tutsi. The international community was shaken. Graphic descriptions and shocking photographs of what happened in Rwanda in April-June 1994 appeared in the international media. But despite this massive publicity no one, to my knowledge, has yet answered the simplest question of all: why did this happen?

Confusion over this most basic issue persists to this day, twelve years after the tragedy. Wherever I go outside Rwanda, ordinary people and officials always ask me the same question: how on earth could you Hutu and Tutsi allow this horrendous, bloody conflict to arise between you? Such questions can only mean that the world still considers what happened a traditional ethnic or tribal conflict—simply one more among a never-ending series of similar conflicts which mark African history. The unparalleled scale of this one only makes people think that Africans in that part of the continent must be particularly cruel.

But this is not true. Alas, no writer or journalist has yet taken the trouble to investigate this tragic phenomenon in its entirety. Everyone repeats the phrase "Rwandan genocide"; but the why of this genocide—by whom, against whom, for what reasons—has escaped the public mind. Otherwise it would be impossible to refer to the Rwandan events of 1994 as "a bloody conflict between Hutu and Tutsi." This is no more accurate than referring to the most dreadful events of World War II as "a bloody conflict between the Nazis and the Jews."

Non-Rwandans may choose to respect the rules of *bon ton*: they may think that touching upon the uncomfortable and delicate points may further split our already torn nation. They prefer to depict the horrors of the genocide and then, invariably, advocate reconciliation. But what of us, the Rwandans? Should we also keep a tactful, no, shameful silence about what all of us know perfectly well in our hearts— namely, that what happened can at any moment begin again?

There is no resource in Rwanda worth more than the inestimable human resources we have already lost. So it is time to put aside superstitions and fears and look back honestly: we must unveil the causes of this tragedy. In the Western world, the collective conscience of the nations emerged from the experience of the Holocaust with a clear understanding of what ethnic cleansing meant. In Rwanda, the same kind of tragedy was followed by—nothing. No one dares to call the plague we suffered by its true name. If doctors choose to hide the causes of an illness from the patient, he has little chance of being cured—and less of staying cured. The next outbreak of the illness will most probably be fatal.

The Western world has long assumed that ethnic strife is but a kind of entrance fee that underdeveloped nations must pay for enjoying the benefits of democracy. The Rwandan tragedy clearly showed that something is wrong with this traditional view. In Rwanda, the massacre was not the result of a quarrel between neighbors, nor was it an ethnic or tribal conflict. It was an organized campaign, prepared by the members of a "democratically" elected government and led by its regular troops. It was, in fact, the direct result of democracy gone wrong. Or, perhaps, an example of how successfully— frighteningly successfully—a democracy can be manipulated. The poor and illiterate make up the overwhelming majority of the citizenry in most African countries. This is an ideal breeding culture for a locally-adapted version of National Socialist-style fascism. Anyone who doubts this should look into the Rwandan experience; those who witnessed it themselves should testify accordingly.

This is why I decided to write this book. I wanted to find in our past the roots of the present tragedy. I cannot claim to be impartial in this matter—no one in Rwanda is. I am Tutsi myself, and I will tell the story from a Tutsi point of view. If others wish to tell the same story from another standpoint, they may try to do so. But one salient fact cannot be omitted from anyone's narrative: in 1994, Tutsis were exterminated in massive numbers, in their own homes, for one reason alone—because they were born Tutsi. Only after this is acknowledged will it be possible to answer the daunting question: why did this happen? If the Tutsis, in fact, harbor something mysterious in them, it is high time to reveal it—and together to dispel the falsehoods and confusion which still surround my people.

Some subjects I touch upon in this book are extremely delicate, to say the least. Many times I found myself hesitating: should I describe this or omit it? Then I would remember those countless Tutsis, watching their death as it approached them, encircled by enemies. The last earthly thought of these souls may well have been: will anyone beyond those here today ever know the truth? That saddening image gave me the courage to complete the account. As the daughter of a beloved father who perished in 1994, and on behalf of all who remain silent forever, I will speak now.

Chapter 1

What Tutsi Means

Most people in the world have no clue as to what the word Tutsi signifies. It is simply a strange-sounding term to many; for others it is a nationality, a tribe or something of that sort. In the face of this all-too-limited recognition, I want to begin with a brief introduction to what it means to be Tutsi.

For Africans it is normal to identify oneself not only by country, but by specific ethnic group (ethnicity) as well. Because national borders in Africa were traced by Europeans with no regard for the distribution of native populations, the map of Africa looks like a party cake sliced up for serving. And Africans traditionally rely much more on their neighbors and relatives than on their governments. Ethnicity in Africa provides a natural framework for survival, a means toward the end of daily assistance in one's life. As everywhere in the world, a common language and common traditions naturally link people to one another; in poor nations that link is stronger. One is hard pressed to name a single country in Africa where people do not place a high value on their ethnicity and do not use it to identify themselves.

Each country can usually count several ethnicities. Some of them are small; in the Congo, for example, linguists have counted some 250 different languages (which has made communication among the Congolese dependent on a kind of French). In other regions, ethnicities live less compactly and often on either side of national borders. So people of different countries may feel, regardless of their citizenship, that they are of the same ethnicity. Scholars call this a reminiscence of the primitive structure of society; some politicians baldly term it "tribalism."

Upon hearing that word, many modern Westerners

immediately think of scenes from films like Lara Croft's *Tomb Raider*. The intrepid white woman, trapped by half-naked black savages (whose chief is dressed in some kind of feather costume)…but you get the idea. Many times I have watched astonished Europeans and Americans during their initial arrival in Africa (as a human resources officer, I often went to Kigali airport to meet people there.) Foreigners look around warily, searching for evidence that they have really arrived in "wild" country. At length, after finally catching sight of some half-naked black bodies in leopard skins—in a band of traditional dancers at a hotel or in a restaurant, for example— the newcomers seem reassured. Such is the power of outdated clichés, even among educated people. In fact, we Rwandans do not walk around naked, and we do not wear animal skins; we are people very much like you. We have our poverty, just as Westerners do; but even our poorest peasant in the faraway border lands still has a pair of trousers. He sits in a proper manner on his hand-made chair next to his small house. On Sundays he puts on a shirt and a wool jacket (second-hand, of course) and goes to church with his wife. I have never seen half-naked people in our churches, or people dressed in Bermuda shorts, for that matter—as one sometimes sees in Europe. And it is rather hotter at midday in African churches than in European ones, I might point out…

To be honest, I doubt that the distinction between ethnicity and nationality is limited to Africans. If one looks at the Germans—not as former colonizers abroad, but at home in Europe—one finds, for example, that a Bavarian may display much more dedication to his region than to his country, and may well prefer his fellow-Bavarians to all other Germans. One need hardly mention, moreover, the importance of not accidentally calling a Scotsman an Englishman. Nor is it easy to dismiss the signs one sees posted in public venues in the very midst of educated, bilingual Belgium: "This is a Flemish territory. Please speak Flemish." I cannot remember ever seeing a sign like this in Africa… Perhaps ethnic feelings, for good and ill, are the same in whites and Africans, with only the local temperament and material standing differentiating them. That said, it follows that to call African ethnicities "tribes" is at least as misleading as to use this term for citizens of developed nations—to describe, say, southern Germans as the "Bavarian tribe", or to say that Canada is populated by two major "tribes"—the English and French—and a number of smaller ones: Chinese, Poles, Ukrainians…

So Tutsi is not a tribe and not a nationality; Tutsi is an ethnicity. This ethnicity has historically lived in the region of east Africa situated between two mighty African lakes, Tanganyika and Victoria. They have inhabited not only Rwanda, but also Burundi, the southern neighbor of Rwanda. Since I am Rwandan, I write mainly of Rwandan Tutsis, even though this book sometimes deals with the ethnicity as a whole.

In Rwanda, Tutsis live together with another ethnicity, the Hutu: Tutsi are the minority and Hutu the majority. Another ethnicity is also found here, the Twa, or Pygmies; but they now number only a fraction of one percent of the total population. The same distribution of ethnicities obtains in modern Burundi. But this does not mean that two countries were formerly one, and were artificially split apart by the colonialists (as was often the case in Africa). On the contrary: Rwanda and Burundi were split long ago in historical terms; when Western explorers came to the region, they found two separate kingdoms. The Belgians tried to fuse both kingdoms together into a single colonial state, Ruanda-Urundi, for easier administration; but this never worked, and after independence both states once again resumed their separate existences.

The mother tongue of all Rwandans is a rich and splendid language, Kinyarwanda. Differing slightly from the language of our neighbors in Burundi, Kinyarwanda is uniform within our country: no linguist can detect any discrepancies in pronunciation between Tutsi and Hutu speakers. In addition, intellectuals in Rwanda, regardless of their origins, universally speak French or English (and often both). Neither does religion distinguish Tutsi and Hutu: the proportion of Catholics, Protestants and Muslims in both ethnicities is the same. For centuries Tutsi, Hutu and Twa lived as neighbors, always in close proximity: a field of one reached the pasture of another. Unlike other countries, such as Belgium, Rwanda never had whole provinces of one or another ethnicity. And just as we share our land, religion and language, so we also share our history. If one starts to speak about himself, he must immediately pronounce the name of the other.

What is it, then, that makes us so unmistakably identify ourselves as Tutsi? Why, by the same token, do our neighbors just as clearly identify themselves as Hutu? There has never been a geographical boundary between us; yet there has been a boundary—a boundary in our minds. The distinction between us is thus at once ephemeral and clear-cut; to understand it, one must look to our past.

Chapter 2

Where the Tutsi Came From

We do not know anything of the origins of the Tutsi. One may suppose, judging by their more or less mythical oral accounts, that they first appeared in the 13th or 14th century, first in the west, then in the center, then slowly progressed towards the east of the country [Rwanda]. But these questions of origin do not hold any real interest at all. After all, what are the Belgians, what are the French? At play in these is a mixture of German, Gallo-Roman and other sources; in the end, no one challenges our anthropological origins from the physical point of view.
Luc de Heusch

All who have visited our country are agreed: if an earthly Paradise were ever to exist, it would have to be located somewhere near Rwanda. It is in this region of the Rift Valley that the oldest human remains have been discovered, and no wonder. For here man's earliest ancestors found springs of clean mountain water; an abundance of green leaves; lovely sunshine; refreshing rains; a climate of pleasant days and gently cooling nights. God gave all this to our land not for a short summer season, but for the whole year. With our fertile soil we enjoy up to three harvests in a calendar year. This land has always yielded enough food to feed all its children. The country is not large in terms of territory; its land extends not horizontally but gently upward: Rwanda was long ago called, and quite rightly, "the land of a thousand hills." Our mountains are not forbidding, they are inhabited—nearly all of them.

We have no access to the sea, and from the north, the west and the east the country is surrounded by imposing neighbors: Uganda, Congo and Tanzania. Only to the south does our border link us with another small country, Burundi. This has had a significant impact on the character of our people. Not accustomed to seeing great open spaces around them, Rwandans have always been a people familiar with hidden pathways, unexpected traps and sudden danger. So we are not a straightforward people. We carefully select words and teach children not to display emotions. Those who know us superficially may take this reticence as a sign of innate hypocrisy. Others would say that it really speaks more to long tradition as shepherds and watchmen. This is closer to the truth. A Tutsi is one who instinctively mistrusts frankness and genuinely dislikes boldness: among our neighbours we have the reputation of an extremely reserved people. We owe this not only to our geography, but also to our history.

Up until the colonial period there was no written history of Rwanda. But this does not mean that there was no history at all. Like the ancient Greeks and the Jews, for centuries the Rwandans preserved the record of their past in an elaborate oral tradition. The twenty-first century mind can hardly comprehend this: how, we now wonder, could the entire book of Genesis have been memorized word-for-word? Yet it passed down from father to son for more than a thousand years before it was finally set down in writing. That art of memorization has been all but abandoned by modernity. But only fifty years ago, a favorite competition among young men at the royal court of Rwanda was reciting by heart, in front of the entire assembly, a historical poem lasting nearly three hours! What made the competition sporting was that all the noble listeners themselves knew the poem by heart from their youth: thus the young declaimer could not afford to misquote more than a single verse. The punishment for a second error was to be shunned by the king and his retinue, and to be effectively banned from a political career. The reward for a successful declamation, on the other hand, was commensurately high: a cow from the royal herd and the prospect of becoming one of the King's trusted officers. Our history was thus engraved in our national mind more deeply than if it had been carved in stone.

I never heard this wonderful poem; my parents did. And my grandfather still knew it by heart as a very old man. The genealogy reconstructed from that poetic source indicates that Rwanda became a centralized monarchy beginning in the 13th century. Not many European dynasties can boast a history this ancient, and we Rwandans are rightfully proud of our venerable antiquity. I will also note—only for purposes of clarifying the particulars of this account—that all sovereigns on that list, from the first to the last, belonged to the Tutsi ethnicity. The table on the page 20 shows the dynasty of Rwandan sovereigns.

For many thousands of years our fertile hills were an open field for the natural struggle for survival: human beings appeared here long before they expanded towards Europe, Asia, and then on to America and Oceania. At first human density in the territory was so low that the primitive communities freely moved from location to location, staying at whichever they found safest. It is hard to tell now, in examining this earliest of eras, whether distinctions among Hutu, Tutsi and Twa already existed; perhaps not. In modern ethnography it is widely accepted that ethnicities are a relatively late product of migration, mixture and assimilation. But whenever they appeared here, one thing seems certain: each ethnicity must have started from only a small number of native ancestors. This can be deduced from the fact that even today all three are physically different from each other. Tutsis are typically tall and thin; Hutus are usually a bit shorter but noticeably more muscular; and Twa are clearly of diminutive stature, flexible and sinuous. Each ethnicity grew in number while maintaining its identity largely through endogamous marriage. And all the three shared the rich territory, each specializing in different areas of the primitive economy—or so we must assume, as otherwise it is impossible to explain why they coexisted rather than eliminating one another as competitors.

Table: The Dynasty of Rwandan Sovereigns

Mythical predecessors:
Kijuru—Kobo—Merano—Randa—Gisa—Kizira—Kazi—and
other kings said to have "come from heaven"

Historical kings ruling Rwanda from approximately 1280 to 1961:
- Kanyarwanda I Gahima
- Yuhi Musindi
- Rukuge
- Nyarume
- Rumeza
- Rubanda
- Ndahiro I Ruyange
- Ndoba
- Samembe
- Nsoro I Samukondo
- Ruganzu I Bwimba
- Cyirima I Rugwe
- Kigeri I Mukobanya
- Mibambwe I Mutabazi
- Yuhi II Gahima
- Ndahiro II Cyamatare
- Ruganzu II Ndoli
- Mutara I Semugeshi
- Kigeri II Nyamuheshera
- Mibambwe II Gisanura
- Yuhi III Mazimpaka
- Karemera Rwaka
- Cyirima II Rujugira
- Kigeri III Ndabarasa
- Mibambwe III Sentabyo
- Yuhi IV Gahindiro
- Mutara II Rwogera —
- Kigeri IV Rwabugiri —
- Mibambwe IV Rutarindwa —
- Yuhi V Musinga —
- Mutara III Rudahigwa —
- Kigeri V Ndahindurwa

Which group was the first to appear in Rwanda? This question suddenly obtained a new importance about fifty years ago—not as a point of scientific interest, but in a purely political context. A great deal of speculation was launched on the subject. Without entering into this discussion, I must say that my own assumption is that the Twa must have been the first; because the Twa were mainly primitive hunters, the Tutsi were cattle-breeders and the Hutu were farmers. To start either farming or cattle breeding one must first cut down the dense primitive forest.

> The genealogical traditions [in all the regions of Rwanda] indicate that the earliest progenitors of the indigenous lines had once cleared the forest land where their descendants came to live. With unhesitating certainty these descendants declare themselves as having originated from Hutu or Tutsi ancestors. It will suffice to recall that the clearing of the land and its subsequent settlement took place at the same time and on the same hills by both Tutsis and Hutus.... Where exactly did one or the other come from? For how long did they live in the region which later became Rwanda? No known documentation provides an answer to these questions. One thing, however, confirms the two groups' longstanding coexistence: they share one and the same language.
> *Claudine Vidal*

So where exactly did the Tutsi come from? They did not have to come from anywhere. Or, more exactly, even if their patriarchal ancestors came from somewhere specific, this location remains forever shrouded in myth. For as far as the human mind can penetrate into the past, the Tutsi have always lived in Rwanda—as have the Hutu and Twa. In all likelihood, all three emerged as ethnicities in the region of the Great African Lakes. All three with equal right consider this beautiful land their patrimony. Historical records offer only very early reports of struggles for power among the chiefs of the primitive communities prior to the appearance of the

21

centralized kingdom. After a single ruler—a Tutsi king—was enthroned, his subjects, of different ethnic backgrounds, stopped fighting among themselves. In time of war, all three groups joined to defend the country in the king's army. In times of peace, the three had even less reason to compete: each had a specific social role to play and each needed the others as partners.

In other words, Tutsi, Hutu and Twa are all authentic indigenous groups, part and product of traditional Rwandan society. Let us now turn to the inner structure of this society: a knowledge which is essential for a real understanding of this people.

Chapter 3

Tutsi in the Traditional Society

The first missionaries gave the word "noble" as a synonym for "Tutsi."
Jean-Luc Chavanieux

Fifty years ago, in our grandparents' day, membership in a specific economic class was what primarily distinguished the ethnicities in Rwanda. Almost without exception, a Twa boy endeavored to learn the thousand-year-old secrets of hunting from his father. Necessarily, by the time he reached his majority, he was already an accomplished pathfinder and sharpshooter. A young man born in a Hutu family, by contrast, knew from childhood that he would most likely become an agricultural laborer or an artisan—because all of his ancestors had been. Finally, a young Tutsi was prepared to raise cattle—not only to follow the centuries-long Tutsi tradition, but also for a practical reason: he would inherit a share of his father's livestock.

But cattle are a fragile asset. They can be killed by wild animals, stolen, or caught up by disease and their numbers thus greatly reduced (or eliminated altogether). Very often, a Tutsi father's livestock was not sufficient to endow all the sons in the family. In such cases, an alternative for young Tutsi males was professional military service. Over the passage of time, this became a tradition. Other occupations, such as commercial trade, were less popular among our ethnicity. Of course, today we have many successful businessmen; but it is still fair to say that a love of money has never figured in the profile of the genuine Tutsi. In Rwanda, regular (minted) money was introduced in virtually compulsory fashion by the Belgians only in the twentieth century. Prior to that a cow had satisfactorily played the role of monetary unit. In any case, I

23

think it is appropriate to offer here my view: state service is a Tutsi's true vocation and his proper element. An innate self-discipline is Tutsi's most singular strength.

I remember an old photograph showing a military exercise conducted by Tutsi soldiers. Armed with spears, bows and light bucklers, these warriors, mobile and noiseless, had a reputation of never tiring and never complaining. In the picture, two of them are standing in front of a cohort, with a spear horizontally resting on their shoulders between one and another. Their comrades are preparing to jump over the spear; one already jumping is fully armed, face up, ready to attack his enemy straight after landing.

What was the place of the Tutsi in traditional Rwandan society, and what was their relationship with other ethnicities? Beyond the king himself—who was invariably a Tutsi—the highest officials in the state hierarchy were Tutsi as well. Most of these officials were directly linked to the king by blood, and were in fact his relatives. This was possible because of an ancient belief that the king was a kind of a other-worldly being, a creature to whom the usual matrimonial norms and restrictions did not apply; thus during his numerous inspection travels throughout the country, and as a special honor to a given family, the king could spend the night with any unmarried girl. If the girl then became pregnant by the king, it was in no way regarded as a dishonor to the family. On the contrary, all concerned awaited the king's child with joy. Later, many of these handsome young princes, brought up by their grandparents, arrived at the royal court and made their careers there. Naturally, they had to confirm their nobility by demonstrating good manners and personal courage. Usually, a new ruler was chosen from among the sons of the deceased monarch, and was proclaimed king by a close group of influential courtiers. Thus dynastic succession was determined by both the closest blood relationship (father-to-son) and, even more tellingly, by the political weight behind the different candidates.

I should note here that generally in Rwandan tradition, a girl's pregnancy before marriage was totally unacceptable. In fact, it was strictly punished: the poor sinner was publicly condemned to death, but not executed. She was removed to the distant forest wilds and abandoned there to God's mercy. Most were then killed by animals, but some did survive. Each of us Tutsi girls knew from childhood: the only hope for such a poor soul was to be found by the Twa Pygmies and to spend the rest of her life with them, in their forest shelters. Even today, our youngsters seem to me to hold much more conservative views about sexual behavior than do their European counterparts. Most girls maintain a proper decency (at least superficially) and will go to great lengths to avoid disreputable rumors. For better or worse, the age of kings travelling through Rwanda and visiting maidens at night has also passed.

The Tutsi-Twa relationship was always one of mutual trust. Strikingly different from the Tutsi in appearance, the Twa, like the Tutsis, were a minority. Up until the abolition of the monarchy in 1961, Twa archers always served as personal bodyguards to the Tutsi king. The sovereigns appreciated their loyalty and uncompromising commitment. Now the Twa live in Rwanda in small communities, happy to maintain their traditions and rites and mostly marrying among themselves. While there are no more forests for hunting, Twa men have become outstanding artisans and professional dancers. The diminutive Twa ladies are known as the best potters in Rwanda. Once in a while they would knock at your door with their wares, offering lovely and practical Rwandan round pots at very modest prices. I studied with one Twa boy in the last classes of college; he was a serious and dependable young man who stood only about one and a half meters high. When our Tutsi boys all left for the front to free Rwanda by force of arms, he too went to front with them. I never saw him again. In Kigali, I knew one prominent journalist who was a native Twa; but beyond exceptions like these one sees few Twa in daily life. But let us return to the ancient traditions.

25

> The society of classes had the tendency to become a society of castes, marked by a marked endogamy: Tutsi aristocrats reproduced themselves through endogamous marriages and ended up creating a kind of phenotype, at least partially distinguishing them from the Hutu masses.
> *Luc de Heusch*

Just think: people consciously created of themselves a kind of phenotype, which distinguished them by height, posture, facial shape, manners, and so on. How did they accomplish this? One might assume that Tutsi family traditions of good manners may at least have played a role. For example, a true Tutsi, seeking to feed himself, will not eat his food anywhere; he will know the importance of a proper time and place for everything. Among the skills we children were taught by parents was a disregard for hunger: we were supposed not to show a weakness for food, and were made to feel that one may even live with no food at all. If a child drank enough cow's milk, the parents usually would not show great concern about his health; in Rwandan tradition it is widely accepted that milk contains everything a child needs. The adults chose their food in a unique way as well.

> A part of each lunch and dinner should be meat, fish or eggs, to provide enough iron and proteins; and each meal should further include dairy products to provide both sufficient calcium and adequate quantities of proteins and vitamins... Finally, there should be cooked or fresh vegetables and one fruit for vitamins.
> *The French Nutritional Research and Information Center, 2001.*

As I read that perfectly balanced European diet, I immediately recalled the traditional food of my parents and grandparents: beef, cheese, a kind of butter called *amavuta'yinka*, fresh and fermented milk, and always fruit and vegetables. To me, this is one of the explanations behind both the unique physical appearance of the Tutsis and the famous beauty of our ladies—a beauty which lasts to a very advanced age. Our forebears knew these secrets and preserved them for generations.

I have spent a great deal of time with our old Tutsi ladies, trying to learning from them the secret of how to raise a child correctly—one who will became a true Tutsi without a blemish. I have come to understand one thing: that this cannot be done outside the unique environment which served as the cradle of Tutsi ethnicity. Certain elements are irreplaceable: the Rwandan air they breathed; the Rwandan water they drank; the Rwandan pastoral scenes they admired. No less important were the stories they heard from their grandparents. And beyond these, Tutsi mothers carefully and tirelessly performed on their infants a special kind of massage; young men practiced certain specific exercises unique to the Tutsi; youngsters were praised or criticized by adults in a precise and peculiar Tutsi way.

> ...To be a Tutsi meant to belong to a dominating class, to posses cattle, to exercise a political function, or to have as dependants a certain number of Hutu clients. These signify social distinctions rather than racial ones.
> *Luc de Heusch*

Is this entirely true? Were all Tutsis aristocrats? Far from it. Most who were Tutsi by birth were born—and remained—simple peasants. And a simple Tutsi did not enjoy particular privileges over a simple Hutu: if he had no cattle, he would become a servant or a soldier, exactly as would a simple Hutu who had no land to cultivate. Both perished equally for their country in military campaigns. It was mainly the Tutsis of high social status who had access to administrative positions—access not available to their rich Hutu counterparts. This is what really made Rwandan society a feudal one.

Another important point can be raised in connection with this "society of castes": a person who was Hutu by birth might one day become a Tutsi—and this transformation would

27

thereafter apply to all his descendants! Usually this was a reward for outstanding personal courage, or for rendering a particularly important service to the king. Consider the situation: the king publicly proclaims that a certain person, from this day forward, will belong to another ethnicity; that person then feels changed forever, even though the shape of his nose obviously remained the same. Does this not resemble honorary nobility rather than an ethnicity-based one? Paradoxical as it may seem to an outside observer, for us Rwandans there is nothing astonishing in this. We have always felt that our ethnic difference is something not so much biological as traditional.

A Western reader not familiar with Africa may think that our feudal society was simply a replica of the European feudalism of five hundred years earlier. But this is not the case. Europeans developed their feudalism after three thousand years of living in a temperate climate and through many innovations: stone and wooden constructions which could be inherited by descendants; the stockpiling of agricultural products in wintertime, and the exchange of these products for durable goods; and finally, the use of money for exchange. All these factors had the ancillary effect of furthering the accumulation of wealth. European feudal lords could allow themselves certain luxuries: living in splendid palaces, eating from silver plates, and keeping themselves apart from their vassals. They were separated from their people by stone walls, removable bridges and armies of servants and guards; lords and vassals were linked mainly through taxes, requisitions and duties.

Now consider, by comparison, the feudal society which the Germans found when they came to Rwanda. The country lies on the equator; there is no change in climate the year round, except during the three months when there is no rain. Consequently, there are three harvests a year. There is no way and no need to stockpile agricultural products: if they are not consumed in time, heat, humidity and rodents will destroy them in any case. The country's economy was self-sufficient; no trade was developed because virtually none was needed. To their astonishment, the arriving Germans found no money in use in the country—for the simple reason that there was no need for it; consequently, there was no need for units of weight and measure! The colonialists certainly thought that these lacunae derived from desperate underdevelopment, but such was not the case. Anyone who knows our culture can confirm this: the lack of such instruments indicated not backwardness, but a different system of values and priorities. For example, in our language, Kinyarwanda, one can express the finest nuances of human relationships, psychology and moral categories; many of these expressions do not have adequate equivalents in the three European languages I know. On the other hand, certain material terms are simply not represented.

This means that not only the lifestyle but also the philosophy of Rwandan feudal society was markedly different from their European counterparts. In our culture much more importance was given to traditions based on arbitrary human agreement than to those relying on formal laws. This was normal for a society which knew no writing and preserved the national culture in living memory rather than on paper or stone. Such a culture may at first glance seem unproductive; but it is simply productive in a different way. True, natural barter required rather more time than trade involving money; but our ancestors had this time. Take, for example, a typical deal between a Tutsi nobleman and a Hutu peasant. The peasant wants a cow; or additional land, or protection against neighbors; or some other good or service. There is one avenue open to him to obtain all these: through a powerful Tutsi aristocrat. The peasant explains his request to one of the Tutsi's subordinates and asks for an appointment; then he brings products from his household: bunches of bananas, panniers of flour, pots of homemade sorghum beer or banana wine. The nobleman looks into the Hutu's request and decides to accept or not accept the gifts. If the decision is positive, the peasant becomes a client of the feudal squire: from then on he enjoys the latter's help and protection, for which he must, from time to time, bring further gifts. If the squire's decision is negative and he does not accept the gifts, the seeker may wait a decent interval, then come a second time with more gifts—or he may choose to go with the same request to another member of the gentry.

Obviously, once accepted as a feudal vassal the peasant was no longer free to act against the will of his gentry protector; he had to accompany him on his journeys and serve as his attendant in time of war. But he was free to seek another patron if he was not happy with the way he was treated. If the client family was in trouble or faced starvation, the squire would usually help with his own means. These relationships resembled much more a patriarchal clan, with the gentry playing the role of clan head, than the classical model of European feudal arrangements. The more clients the squire had, the more influential and powerful he was; subsequently, he had more bananas or sorghum beer in any harvest season. But what could he do with all that beer, if he could not drink it all himself, sell it, or stockpile it for the future use? The only solution was to offer it back to the clients who served him, or to potential new ones who appeared at his door with their petitions.

As one can readily perceive, there was no marked difference in lifestyle among the members of this society. Not only the feudal gentry but the king himself lived in the same kind of bamboo hut, as all of his subjects, only more beautiful and larger in size. (And by the way: there is no better and more comfortable accommodation in our climate than the traditional Rwandan *urugo*, the round wattle bamboo house. Protecting its inhabitants from sunshine and tropical rains, the *urugo* had the further advantages of being both mobile and hygienic, because it could be easily dismantled and erected from new material in a different place.)

Picture1: In such bamboo-and-straw houses (urugo) Rwandans have lived for centuries. One cannot find urugo houses in modern Rwanda any longer.

The rulers and the vassals ate essentially the same food, though the Tutsis consumed more beef than the Hutu peasants, who traditionally ate sheep and goat. The rulers dressed in imported Arab textiles, while the peasants enjoyed simple homemade wear; but both walked on foot and shunned footwear all their lives. Why didn't the nobility ride? For the simple reason that horses never survived in Rwanda because of their susceptibility to illness. Thus horse-drawn carriages, a staple of human transport elsewhere, were unknown in Rwanda.

I recall once hearing a story on this theme: some well-intentioned whites decided to introduce horse transport into our country. They set up a kind of factory to teach peasants how to manufacture carriages and harness the animals. The workers were enthusiastic and produced a lot of carriages — but only as long as the whites continued to pay them for this job. Once the white bosses decided that the initial stage was over, and it was time for the project to become self-sufficient, not one more carriage was manufactured: nobody wanted to buy them. To this day you will be hard pressed to find a donkey or a horse in the entirety of our national territory (excepting the equestrian club in Kigali). Rwandans either carry their bags on their heads, or rent one of the omnipresent Toyota pick-up trucks to move more significant quantities of goods.

Let us return to our historical survey: the power of a feudal ruler in Rwanda was based not so much on his material wealth as on his moral authority. The more clients he had, the more powerful he was; but he could not acquire new subjects for money, because there was no money. The quantity of subjects depended on the way the ruler judged and managed their needs. Personal abilities and skills played a larger role than inherited wealth. I am not attempting to idealize the past of our small and rather exotic African culture—far from it. Yet even in the most developed modern Western democracies, this principle of matching individual merit with social position is not often realized. A parent's money still does very much— perhaps more than anything else—to determine the place a modern Westerner's child will occupy in tomorrow's society.

I learned a good deal about our ancient traditional culture from books. But even before this I had learned much about it from a richer source: the stories and legends recounted by elders. What I heard from them in my childhood is a bit different from what I read later in some sources about "social injustice in feudal Rwanda." I want to be correctly understood: I make no apology for whatever exploitation took place in our past, and would never dream of returning my country to a state of feudal monarchy. I do not claim that this was an ideal social organization or some kind of earthly paradise. All I am saying is that Rwandan feudalism represented a balanced society, one in which each member had a particular role and place. And at the very least the lives of members of the community were protected. The guarantee lay in the sacred authority of common law accepted by all. Tutsi never killed Hutu and Hutu never killed Tutsi; this lasted for untold generations. When the colonialists abolished this traditional rule of law, claiming it was "defective", they could not replace it with anything nearly as efficient.

I learned many of the details of traditional Rwandan life from the simple, everyday stories which girls usually hear from their mothers. While women in ancient Rwanda did not inherit the father's estate, traditionally they were considered to be carriers of a noble inheritance—a valued resource for subsequent generations. Because my mother came from a family of gentry of the second degree, I often asked her about the way the Hutu and Tutsi used to live before the revolution. This is what she told me: any Hutu, just like any Tutsi, could at any time come to her father's patrimony, the *urugo*, with any claim. All problems were resolved with fairness and decency, and without undue haste. If necessary, representatives of the opposing side—witnesses or simply respected adults—could be invited to the hearing. In any case, the moral authority of such a court was so high that quarrels among neighbors were usually summarily settled on the spot: a judgment would be made, for example, stipulating that the respondent should pay the claimant several cows or goats, or a few pots of traditional beer. The adjudication would be marked by a shared drink of the latter; and that was the end of the dispute.

On the paternal side, my father came from a Tutsi family that did not belong to the ruling elite, even though they had always owned many cows. His father was a Presbyterian pastor. Christian traditions exclude any caste or class prejudices, so in our house ethnic identity was hardly even mentioned. I do not remember any sense of ethnic pride vis-à-vis other ethnicities; on the contrary, the house was always open to all manner of different people, and we children were usually not aware of who was who.

Another example of the almost biblical relationships that prevailed in Rwanda's past is that of master and servant. As I mentioned before, a typical reward for work performed was a cow, because the cow represented both sustenance and a functional monetary unit. As such the cow was not only a symbol of a certain level of prosperity, but also the standard dowry that a family claimed for a girl to be given away in marriage. So it was common to see young men, both Tutsi and Hutu, coming to an elder's *urugo* in search of a job which could bring them a cow, the most highly-valued reward. There was no such thing as forced labor in Rwanda; on the contrary, it was considered great good fortune to be taken into a gentry household as an *umugaragu*, or servant. Along with the pre-arranged payment for his services, a diligent worker also got the opportunity to show his abilities and make a further career for himself. It was customary, of course, for Hutu servants to look up to their masters; but exactly the same was also expected of Tutsi servants.

Yes, it was a feudal society. But each member of this society, finding its laws reasonable and natural, obeyed them. No one ever dreamed of overturning the ancient traditions. This state of affairs continued through the late 1950's, when traditional Rwandan society disappeared forever. But it was some sixty years prior to that time that Rwanda had broken the near-total isolation of its authentic development. It stepped into the larger arena of the modern world—when the Europeans, at length, made their way to what had been the remotest country of the Dark Continent. Since that time relationships among the three ethnicities in Rwanda have been influenced, and often dramatically, by this new factor: the presence of the whites.

Chapter 4

Encountering the Whites

Up until the end of the 19th century, our country remained the last blank area on the maps of the world which children studied in geography lessons at school. The beginning of the end of this "blank space" came in 1858, when the intrepid British explorer John Hanning Speke made mention of our land in his journal. This reference was quite candid, because the brave Speke admitted that it seemed unsafe for him to set foot there—so he contented himself with admiring the chain of volcanoes visible from the Tanzanian bank of the river Akagera. Speke's mission was, in fact, to find the source of the river Nile. The Nile at its lower level is a magnificent waterway, but three thousand kilometers away, in the south, it is altogether different—a multitude of streams, each one pouring down from a mountain spring. Little by little, after hundreds of kilometers of separate running, these streams join together. And each stream claims, with its own justice, the proud distinction being of the Source of the Nile.

To our way of thinking, Speke's mission remains unfulfilled to this day—to the continuing satisfaction of tourist agencies in many African countries. In Rwanda, we have a tourist site called "Source of the Nile" where one can, for a very modest sum, admire a lovely little spring. If you follow this spring, the guide affirms with all due seriousness, it will take you all the way to the Mediterranean Sea. But the Ugandans, I should note, also have such a tourist attraction and a hotel with the same name. Burundians are even luckier: in addition to their Hôtel Source du Nil, they have two different springs bearing that name. For that matter, no one knows how many sources of the Nile there are in the Democratic Republic of Congo; but surely they number in the dozens. Africa is big; wherever you go, you can find what you like.

Stymied at the Rwandan border, Speke was obliged to turn south from the Akagera and eventually entered Burundi. There he first encountered Tutsis—and was immediately struck by their great height and fine-featured faces. Even though pitch black, these people somehow reminded Speke of Europeans. We may recall that this happened after many months of travelling through what is now Tanzania—and at a point when Speke was approaching complete exhaustion. In any case, in his account of 1863 Speke suggested that formerly the Tutsis must surely have been Ethiopians, Egyptians, or even Caucasians; he further speculated that they must have followed the Nile from the north upward, looking for its source just as he had. At that time many people thought that whites who remained under the piercing African sun over generations might eventually turn into Negroes... So this brave British officer, after little more than a fleeting glance at the strange people, rather cavalierly termed them "blackened Semites." Curious as it was, this theory was to have a long life. And it was not Europeans, but autochthonous Africans who "rediscovered" Speke's idea a hundred years later. To inspire their uneducated countrymen to chase away their Tutsi neighbors, Hutu nationalists in Rwanda began a campaign of provocative publications and radio broadcasts in which they claimed that those with long legs and fine noses were not actually Rwandans at all—indeed, they were hardly even Africans.

Did these propagandists sincerely believe what they were teaching? Of course not; they simply needed a pretext with which to justify the insanity they were fomenting. And they found one. This is the primary lesson left by John Hanning Speke: one must spend considerable time dealing with African ethnicities before offering judgments about them. Short missions and official interviews are not sufficient for a real appreciation of the nuances involved. And without such a real appreciation, one may find oneself as close to the truth as someone who believes he is admiring the "true" source of the Nile.

But do we Tutsi indeed resemble Ethiopians? The last Belgian Governor-General of Ruanda-Urundi, Jean Paul Harroy, wrote in his memoirs that to him the resemblance was striking. According to Harroy, during his passage through Addis Ababa he nearly mistook several Ethiopians for some of his Tutsi employees. My own experience is different. When I had an opportunity to visit both Ethiopia and Egypt, I decided to look carefully for my (possible) Abyssinian roots. I also looked closely at all the Somalis passing through, because they also live in an adjacent culture of the Nile. In the end I can say unequivocally: I could not find any resemblance between these people and my countrymen. True, some features of Abyssinian faces are not typically Negroid, and thus distinguish Abyssinians from most of the rest of Africa's inhabitants—but what else? The differences between us are much more striking than the similarities. To begin with, these people are much shorter than we are. The Ethiopians are also much more light-skinned. And their overall body structure is completely different. If you took the first Rwandan Tutsi you came across and placed him into the middle of the Suk market in Addis Ababa, he would stand out immediately. The Tutsi would probably seem twice the height of the Ethiopians around him, and his fine-featured construction, flat belly and long arms would likewise distinguish him clearly. Beyond these physical traits, the behavior of the Tutsi—restrained, reserved and polite—would immediately set him apart among the loud, outgoing Ethiopians. (One can only imagine the thoughts of such a misplaced Tutsi, who would probably be wondering what strange and unfortunate twist of fate had put him there!) At all events, while I offer my regrets to those who may feel differently, for me there was no doubt: during my time in Addis Ababa I never felt, even for a moment, as if I were among my ancestors. And I do not think any Tutsi would.

Speke's initial vision of the beautiful green hills of Rwanda did not open our land to the Europeans. In 1871 another British expedition—this one led by Henry Morton Stanley (who in fact was an American)—tried to succeed where Speke had failed. This time the explorers wanted to pass through Rwanda in order to find the source of the Congo River. They finally succeeded in finding this source, but again they did not enter Rwanda: the Stanley expedition was obliged to make a long hook detour to the north, into the territory of modern Uganda. All the entrances to Rwanda were controlled by mighty warriors; these were, as Stanley was given to understand, Tutsis—and they would not let him pass. Stanley's mistake was that he traveled from Zanzibar with an enormous Swahili caravan and Arab interpreters; seeing these, the Rwandan border guards took him for a slave hunter. Stanley, forever linked in the popular mind to the wise Livingstone, should have known: not one single slave was ever abducted from our small mountainous country.

I hold in my hands the two old volumes of nearly six hundred pages each, Stanley's famous *Through the Dark Continent*, issued in London in 1878 (shortly after Stanley's return from Africa). These are remarkable volumes: fine leather covers; expensive paper; detailed plans; elaborate maps; comparative parallel linguistic tables; hundreds of drawings. In that expedition Stanley lost nearly two hundred of his black carriers and five of his white companions. For me, someone who has lived not only in Rwanda, but also in Congo and Burundi, it was a pleasure to read Stanley's masterful descriptions of African nature and peoples. Many of the details around Lake Tanganyika and the Congo River were familiar. But, of course, the descriptions that Stanley dedicated to the Tutsis were of the greatest interest to me.

Not only had the characteristic appearance of the Tutsis struck him. Stanley also found that the tall warriors from both Lake Ihema in the north and Lake Tanganyika in the south were unrivaled diplomats, masters of delicate missions and secret operations. Along with his geographical discoveries, Stanley also made important psychological observations. More than once I laughed aloud at the brave but naive American as he marveled at a Tutsi's clever ruse. Yes, Stanley, you were right: centuries of living among hostile and far outnumbering neighbors certainly taught this people subtlety and stealth.

After the expedition of Stanley, nothing changed in the Great Lakes region. In 1885, the European colonial powers finally decided to stop fighting among themselves in the faraway and hostile continent. At the Berlin conference they agreed to divide Africa up in gentlemanly fashion. The land of Rwanda—which no European had yet visited—was assigned to Germany (along with Burundi, and in addition to the German possessions east of Tanganyika). From that time forward, Rwanda formally became a colony—but only on paper. The country's actual inhabitants had no idea of their colonial status for many years. The king of Rwanda kept ruling the country; he continued to judge, punish and reward his subjects just as he had for centuries. His vigilant troops continued to guard the frontiers. News from and of the rest of the world came but occasionally, with those few Arab merchants who brought goods to the country to trade. Apparently, this was all that Rwanda needed.

Prussian generals in Berlin stared at the map of Africa for another seven years, unable to decide what to do with their new colony. Eventually the situation became scandalous—this "neglect" of the colony could not be allowed to continue. The delicate matter of announcing to the new subjects their colonial status was assigned by the Kaiser not to a military mission, but to a scholar. In 1892, the famous Austrian professor Oscar Baumann, a doctor of philosophy and geography, became the first white man to set foot on the soil of Rwanda. Thus the beautiful green hills unveiled themselves to the world of the whites—but did not surrender the ruler of the country. The main mission of Dr. Baumann remained unfulfilled. He spent four days in Rwanda and conducted certain negotiations; his hope was to convince his Rwandan counterparts of the advantages which co-operation with Germany could bring to the kingdom. But his success at this could hardly have been great, as the white scholar was not received by the Tutsi king. It may be that the titles of the university professor and honorable member of various scientific societies did not impress the self-confident sovereign; or perhaps King Kigeri IV Rwabugiri simply wanted the *bazungu* (the whites in the Kinyarwanda language) to come back a second time with their proposals. They did.

Two years later, in 1894, Count von Götzen arrived in Rwanda as the head of an official mission. This time the German representative was acknowledged as a true ambassador, and the count was received by the king with the all the honor due him. It may bear mentioning, in this context, that von Götzen was accompanied by more than six hundred armed men from the regular German overseas regiment. After crossing the river Akagera, which had stopped so many of their predecessors, the contingent had marched in-country for some days, meeting no resistance. They bivouacked for a period while inquiries were made; finally, messengers brought an invitation to be the king's guests. The ceremonial meeting took place not far from what is today Gisenyi.

The monarch could not boast to his visitors of the splendor of his palace. In fact, there was no palace at all—just a big hut, which could be erected at any place in the kingdom where the sovereign chose to go. The parade and exercises of the royal guard, on the other hand, impressed the guests rather more. The discipline and training on view could have been the envy of a German regiment. For his part, von Götzen did not miss the opportunity to make a good impression on the blacks. A military salute—a simultaneous salvo from 620 Mauser rifles— surely served as effective reinforcement for his commercial proposals and a decisive argument in the negotiations. These rifles could be a fine object for barter in the future, the Rwandans concluded. In the end, the *bazungu* ambassador asked for a small favor: if His Majesty would not mind, the German troops would like to raise a piece of fabric over a big hill nearby, as a symbol of friendship—as was customary among white people. Consent was given, and the Kaiser's flag was sent aloft. Rwanda became a colony.

Perhaps the most important thing the German envoy had understood was that the power of this country consisted not in its material richness, but in the near-deistic authority that the king exercised over his subjects. The sovereign held the power of life and death. To obtain favor in his eyes meant immediate advancement in one's career, while the king's disapproval signaled disaster for the unlucky supplicant. The entire hierarchy of the society was based on discipline and obedience.

> Tutsi and Hutu…respected the same system of laws, and all recognized at the summit of the social pyramid the prestigious power of a sacred King—the Master of nature and of his society.
> *Luc de Heusch*

The tradition of obeying the rulers and submitting oneself to a strict, near-military discipline persists to the present day. Hierarchical structure is the key: in rural areas groups of ten peasants select a first-degree chief, who represents them and who receives the appropriate respect from them. Ten such units make up the next level of organization, and they together select the next chief in the hierarchy; and so on. In this way, the society is both recognizably organized and efficiently manageable.

In a way, this penchant for organization may go some way towards explaining the principal events of Rwandan history in the century which followed the visit of Von Götzen: the peculiarity of colonial rule—which in fact was never complete; the revolution—which was organized and closely assisted; and the subsequent genocide—which was entirely premeditated and a carefully prepared operation.

41

Chapter 5

Colonialism

Such was the state in which the first Westerners encountered Rwanda at the end of the nineteenth century: a clearly feudal society and a genuinely African culture. This traditional social system was intricately balanced and in this sense resembled other balanced systems in nature, like those that form the ecology of a given place. And just as biological systems naturally resist efforts to subvert them, social systems also strive for self-preservation. A region's ecological balance may be destroyed gradually (as with the Aral Sea) or suddenly (as with Chernobyl and its environs), depending on the nature of the destructive factors. The explosion which destroyed the social balance in Rwanda did so in a catastrophic way, clearly—but it did not happen unexpectedly. Nearly sixty years passed from the day the white rulers arrived in Rwanda until the day they left. Over those sixty years the social disaster to come lay in a period of incubation, at the end of which the small patriarchal country was plunged into an unprecedented bloodbath. So before dealing with the tragedy, let us first briefly examine the period of colonization.

The Germans, the first Rwandan colonialists, did not have enough time in place to change the country's social atmosphere in a radical way. As a matter of necessity (and self-preservation), their contingents in Rwanda found it best to rely, in matters political and administrative, on the existing local authority. The country was simply too far afield and too hard to reach to warrant instituting a full-blown colonial regime. As late as 1907 Rwanda still could not count a single regular town or proper road. The commander-in-chief of the German garrison finally chose an arbitrarily point in the geometric center of the country and built his headquarters there; this arbitrary point later became the national capital Kigali.

There is still some evidence of German influence in the country: the word for "school" in Kinyarwanda, for example, is obviously of German origin (*ishule*). Another German contribution to our language is the word "burgomaster", which is how the Rwandans started to call their traditional district rulers sometime in the early 20th century. The first Catholic missions in Rwanda were likewise part of the "German period", as they were installed in 1900 under the first white administration.

In 1914, World War I broke out in Europe, and shortly thereafter the colonialist neighbors—the Belgians in the Congo and the Germans in the East African Territories—started to fight each other in parallel to the war in their home countries. The African subjects of the colonial powers found themselves more than a little surprised. These recent converts to Christianity had difficulty understanding what had happened: why should the whites suddenly start killing each other— contrary to what they have been preaching to us? After the war, in any case, Rwanda "changed ownership": the new rulers were Belgian—as part of the victorious coalition against Germany. They received Rwanda as compensation—and they soon settled themselves in the country for what they assumed would be a long period of colonial rule. The Belgians set about "civilizing" their "underdeveloped" subjects rather more actively than had the Germans. Religion was a part of this effort, as once again the Catholic Church set about proselytizing and expanding its influence among new subjects. In 1922, the Catholic Bishop Msgr. Classe was nominated to Rwanda.

Following the Catholic lead, the Protestant churches also quickly established themselves in Rwanda. The Christianization of the country was facilitated by the traditional monotheism of Rwandans. Our ancient religion was based on the cult of the powerful Supreme Being, Imana – the creator of everything. Besides this, there was a kind of domestic worship of the Ryangombe—the spirits of ancestors, which were supposed to intercede on behalf of the family before Imana. Both Hutu and Tutsi shared the same pagan monotheism, so it was easy for our forefathers to accept the idea of God the Almighty. As the Rev. Elisée Musemakweli recently noted in a sermon at the Presbyterian Church in Kigali, "Rwandans didn't wait for the arrival of Christianity to believe in God."

At all events, Rwanda soon became a noticeably Christian province of Africa. Along with the Catholics, Rwanda today includes numerous Baptist, Methodist, Presbyterian, Adventist and other Christian Churches. There are also hundreds of new non-denominational Christian communities in Rwanda, each having its own leader emerged from their midst. They are typically self-determined and hardly recognize any other spiritual authority but Christ himself. Muslim mosques are also common on the Rwandan landscape, suddenly looming up before one from among the banana trees after a turn in the road. After the tragedy in Rwanda, many people pose a difficult and troubling question: how could this have happened in such a religious country? While there is no easy answer to this, some of our simpler old people say: this was punishment from God for the Ryangombe idols, still preserved in a few Rwandan households...

By the 1930's, the colonial administration and the Catholic Church (through Bishop Classe) represented the country's real political power. The new rulers did not show a great deal of consideration for traditional institutions. The most obvious example of this came in 1931 when King Yuhi V Musinga was summarily dethroned by the colonial administration and a new king installed in his place. This successor was chosen carefully; Msgr. Classe became his personal confessor. And with this accession to the throne, the monarchy in Rwanda became a largely ceremonial institution.

Picture2: Preaching in the open air (1964)

The Belgian administration did not stint in its efforts to develop the new colonial territory as quickly as possible. Their first initiative was to set the local authorities building roads. In places where for centuries there had been no way to pass, road construction, using tens of thousands of mobilized peasants, began to change the country's profile. Thanks to the Belgians, our provinces are now linked by what may be the best traffic network in sub-Saharan Africa. The roads allowed the speedy passage of foodstuffs between provinces during droughts or other natural disasters. In this way the periodic famines in outlying regions of the country could be relieved. Primarily, famines were caused not by shortages of food, but because there was no way to transport food supplies to where they were needed. Road construction was also responsible for the introduction of money into the lives of the peasants: they were paid for their road work with colonial money. This in turn allowed them to pursue small businesses (instead of barter operations) and to accumulate capital for the first time in their lives.

As one would expect, such significant changes in the nation's lifestyle — over the course of but a single generation — could not take place without controversy. The colonial administration would not have been able to institute all these reforms had it not relied for assistance on the existing resource of authority: the traditional Tutsi gentry. The feudal hierarchy which the Belgians found in place was only slightly modified; the feudal rulers were simply assigned new administrative posts by the colonial administration, while maintaining their traditional privileges. The gentry's children were naturally the first to be sent to schools and seminaries; these young Tutsi became the first generation of Rwandan intellectuals. Perhaps it was at this time that the insidious evil took root. To help assure their control over the population, the colonialists declared the Tutsi closer to Europeans than other Africans. The Hutu, by this logic, were an opposite type — Bantu, true African Negroes — and thus kind, inflexible and simple. It is hard to say at this point whether such favoritism of one ethnicity over another was a premeditated policy of the colonial administration (in accordance with the Roman precept "Divide and rule") or merely a simplification to further organizational ends. Whatever the intention, in any case, the result was enormously socially destructive. The negative energy of ethnic intolerance began to accumulate in Rwanda under colonial rule — specifically, when the white rulers finally began themselves to demolish this social order.

> Throughout the colonial management there was an omnipresent obsession with race; this pleased the whites and transfixed the first generation of literate blacks—inflating the arrogance of Tutsi, considered Europeans with black skin, and frustrating the Hutu, who were treated as Bantu Negroes.
> *Jean Pierre Chrétien*

Most of my countrymen who witnessed this period in our history tend to express their feelings more simply: "It was the colonialists who brought this division to Rwanda." In fact, in the mid-1950s a new colonial policy was put in place. At that time, the Belgians themselves were going through considerable political turmoil at home: after years in opposition, the Belgian Socialists finally came to power, partly on the basis of their criticism of the previous government's inefficient colonial policy. And indeed, the small overseas territory now provided the newly-empowered Socialists a good opportunity to demonstrate their more egalitarian ideals. Under this new approach, Hutu youngsters started to replace the Tutsis in great numbers in the seminaries and in the university faculties. This turnover both polarized the society and provided the first generation of Hutu intellectuals, who in the years to come would assume a new role.

The Belgians decided to rely on the race which they had previously described as "inferior", inflaming the struggle and supporting ethnic antipathies with the aid of the Catholic Church.

> In 1957, the "Ba-Hutu Manifesto", published with the participation of the Catholic Church, termed the Tutsis a "foreign minority race" who had come from Abyssinia and who exploited the "authentic Rwandans", that is the Hutus.
> *Thierry Leftmaster*

In November 1959, a new transitional regime was put into place in Rwanda. It intended to facilitate the transfer of traditional administrative positions from colonial administrators to representatives of political associations and parties. But, as the political parties in Rwanda at that time were mostly associations for the promotion of the "Ba-Hutu Manifesto", the reform had the effect of practically expelling the Tutsis from the political process altogether.

Only yesterday a distinct elite—urbanized, cultivated and favored by their white bosses—the high-ranking Tutsis overnight found themselves marginalized. Suddenly they emerged as nothing more than owners of a few cattle in the hinterlands. For many this represented a personal tragedy. Much more important to the nation as a whole, however, was the fact that this event marked the onset of an "ethnic revolution." One should not lose sight of a fine point here: this revolution both started and came to its successful end while the colonial administration was still in place.

Chapter 6

The Assisted Ethnic Revolution

I think this violence is a product of de-colonization and not of the traditional Rwandan society.
Luc de Heusch

The Rwandan revolution of November 1959 was indeed an insurrectional phenomenon "sous tutelle" (under supervision), followed by a phase of "assisted revolution" lasting several months.
Jean-Paul Harroy

The White Fathers and the Belgian Christian Workers' Movement pushed the "Hutu revolution..."
De Leftmaster

Every revolution, regardless of the goals set for it, at some point turns ugly—through its methods, its consequences or both. History knows no exceptions. Revolutionaries of all stripes—Cromwell, Robespierre, Kropotkin, Lenin and so on— have always considered the shedding of blood an unavoidable necessity, a kind of a breaking of eggs to make the omelet of social justice. But even in the context of the high price in blood which humanity has paid for its revolutions (or "historical advancement"), the revolution in Rwanda of 1959-1962 stands out as something curious and exceptional. While it was ostensibly directed against a feudal economic class, it was in fact from the beginning overtly framed as a revolution of a "suppressed" ethnicity against a "dominating" one; economic considerations became secondary. Beyond this, as we have seen in the previous chapter, the revolutionary wrath itself was to a great extent the result of provocation on the part of the colonial administration. And whereas it took place in a country of near-total illiteracy, the revolution was planned and financially assisted by very well educated people. In fact it was the instrument by which Belgium, anticipating its inevitable departure from the scene, attempted to assure political control over the ex-colony in the future.

Compare this revolution with the events in France which began in 1789, or with the English revolution of the time of Cromwell: in both these cases the revolutionary masses felt that the aristocrats enjoyed unjustified social privileges which should be wrested from them by force. Note the difference and the delicacy of the situation in Rwanda: all the aristocrats were Tutsi; thus to struggle against unjustified privileges meant to struggle against the Tutsi. If in feudal England all the nobility had been of Scottish heritage, igniting a revolution would have entailed the use of blatantly anti-Scottish propaganda. And what if the Scots did not have their own territory, but were dispersed among the population all over the British Isles? Such was the situation of the Tutsis in Rwanda of 1959.

One member of my family recalled how it was in those years, and how it started in 1959. He was then a young child. His whole family—he and his brothers, sisters and parents— together began to hear loud shouting by Hutu activists at night; they tried to unnerve the Tutsis by threatening to kill them all, man, woman and child. Soon the threats started to take on reality. Each morning brought news that one or another Tutsi family had been found slaughtered; the burning of Tutsi houses became a regular event. Tutsis' cattle were mercilessly slaughtered as well. Sometimes only a cow's legs would be hacked off with a machete, making the animal's death inevitable yet frightfully agonizing.

Step by step a campaign of stalking the Tutsis was set in motion, in daylight and at night. The stalkers would go from one household to another, searching for Tutsis. At first Tutsi parents sent only their children to hide between the banana trees; later the adults started to hide themselves. From time to time, a family head would leave secretly to forage for food. There was no way to cook, as starting a fire was too risky. And none of the children could make the slightest noise lest their hiding places be revealed. The worst of these scenes came when the Hutu extremists approached at night, carrying torches. It was like being able to watch the end as it slowly approached your family. Indeed, life began to resemble a kind of purgatory, or a waiting room for hell: darkness, rain, mud, silence, the crazed shouting of enemies—and day after day spent in anticipation of a cruel and bloody death. From neighboring hills came the cries of Tutsi victims, the agonized lowing of cattle, and smoke from burning houses. Tutsi aristocrats and Tutsi peasants were killed with no distinction.

Again, all this took place in a country then under Trusteeship (*"sous tutelle"*) of a European power—a power which had both the moral obligation and the military force to restore order. But the Belgians were too heavily engaged in the Congolese turmoil leading up to independence in 1960 to be able to intervene effectively in Rwanda. And in purely practical terms: would it have been possible to intervene on each of Rwanda's thousands of hills? One may send patrols to the streets of the capital city, but soldiers cannot patrol the small paths linking banana fields and cow pastures. Even were soldiers to appear there, whom would they arrest? A peaceful peasant who in the morning cut his sugar cane and in the evening went with the same machete to his neighbor's home?

The extremist element became a movement, growing to massive numbers. They were inspired by demagoguery of the most poisonous sort: "Hutus! You were enslaved for generations! Tutsi foreign invaders took your land! They installed their Mwami [King] over you! Now is your time: away with Mwami! Away with the Tutsi! Their land is yours! Take it, it is lawful, it is not robbery, it is not a sin! If they resist, kill them!" How many poor, illiterate peasants were able to stand firm against such propaganda, with its combination of revenge fantasy and sudden enrichment? For many the temptation to take a neighbor's land was simply too great; exactly how many succumbed to this siren song the devil alone knows. In the end, at all events, the poor did not become rich. The flame of the "holy" war against the Tutsis finally destroyed the country's tiny economy altogether. The only visible result of the campaign for the overwhelming majority of Rwandans was that they now had a number of new leaders who were eager for power and wealth.

A referendum on the future of the king was organized by the colonial administration. The result was predictable: with the new Hutu leaders promising their majority constituency that they would make each Hutu rich and happy after the Mwami was chased away, the king was dethroned. As for the Tutsi politicians, they stubbornly tried to push the clock of history back. With or without the king, they dreamed of preserving their traditional positions as rulers in the context of the new realities; this could be done, they assumed, by creating political parties in the Western manner and mastering the Western parliamentary system. The Tutsi leadership pressed the United Nations to proclaim immediate independence for Rwanda; the quick departure of the whites, they thought, would open the field for a new polity. For a while this became the most important issue for the Tutsi leaders.

Belgium was ready to depart from Rwanda. The discouraging example of the troubled Congo served as an all too clear warning of what might be in store for them elsewhere in Africa. In the Congo, tens of thousands of former colonial households were robbed, and hundreds of whites were raped and murdered. So public opinion in Europe was inclining toward an exit strategy of sorts: let us have done with these colonial adventures and depart. The mood seemed to be: give those Africans their independence if they wanted it.

But surprisingly, the immediate granting of independence to Rwanda was strongly opposed within Rwanda itself. The same new Hutu leaders, who only the day before had been shouting that a republic and not a monarchy was what Rwanda needed, suddenly started to insist on the continuation of the Belgian presence. "Democracy first, then independence" was their slogan beginning in 1960. The Hutus needed the colonial military presence to ensure that all Tutsis of influence would be excluded from the political process. This worked perfectly: the manipulation of nominally democratic procedures among an illiterate feudal population reinforced the Hutu political consolidation and spared the colonialists a second Congo.

For the modern Western reader it may be hard to imagine the process at work here: Rwandan peasants, accustomed for centuries to obeying the rulers, were now told that they must vote. Illiterate, with little idea of what the voting process represented, the suddenly-enfranchised peasantry was easy prey for forceful agitators who told them, in their own language, what should be marked on a ballot. By this time, the Hutu nationalists had already taken complete control of the country's rural areas; and the colonial administration simply assisted the voting process, without any real idea (or the desire to gain one) of the content of the hate propaganda. On July 1, 1962, when the independence of Rwanda was finally proclaimed, the Belgian tricolor was replaced by a Rwandan one and the Governor General handed over power to the first local government. This was not only one hundred percent Rwandan, but also outspokenly Hutu-dominated. The former white rulers left, no doubt with the feeling of having done something good for the people of Rwanda. The "assisted revolution" had triumphed. A seemingly fitting outcome— African control of an African country—had been secured. Even better, this commendable end had been reached, as everyone saw, by the exercise of democracy.

Now, nearly half a century after these events, one can rightfully pose the question: was this democracy? Put otherwise: could real democracy have led to the disaster which was to be visited on Rwanda?

Democracy! Who can speak against you—now virtually a sacred principle? There is perhaps no greater heresy today than to question the validity of democratic procedures. To do so among the progressive people of our time is the same as expressing skepticism about Holy Scripture to an American Baptist, or doubts about the Virgin Mary to a devout Catholic. For that reason I want to make my attitude toward democracy itself perfectly clear: I am sincerely for democracy! (How I longed to see the exercise of free and transparently democratic procedures when I was looking for a job; and how frustrating it was to learn how strong democracy's enemies—partiality and arbitrariness—could be; the effects on human lives of various undemocratic arrangements are discouraging indeed to witness). But to me, coming from a distinctive minority among a much more important majority, another thing is also all too clear: sometimes young democracies ideally suit the ends of dreadful ambitions. As a naive young girl may easily fall victim to a smooth seducer, so a young democracy in Africa—as Europeans themselves had seen on their own continent—could easily fall victim to an ideology based on ethnic intolerance, leading to an overt and fanatic fascism.

But return to the historical question at hand: on balance, did the colonialist-assisted and ethnically-biased revolution of 1959-1962 represent a net gain for the people of Rwanda? Or was it in fact a time bomb certain to explode at some point because it carried the seeds of genocide? In my opinion, our recent history has already answered this question.

The last Belgian Governor General, Jean-Paul Harroy, left his post in 1962. He was fully convinced that he had helped a small nation secure its own well-being for the future. Harroy even titled his memoirs *From Feudalism to Democracy*. After what happened in Rwanda in the decades that followed one would have to add the clause "Through an Ocean of Blood" to the title. Not only did the white bosses betray the Tutsi leaders, whom they had long trusted and honored, but the entire Tutsi ethnicity was put in danger of physical extermination. And even though the white bosses managed to create a Hutu elite before they left, this reward hardly changed the daily lives of the masses of simple Hutu.

One last question can rightfully be posed here: how could such a courageous people as the Tutsis acquiesce not only in their loss of status, but also in the loss of their lives? Was there no armed resistance by the Tutsis? I can only say this: while historically the Tutsis had been warriors, in these new circumstances they were not able to defend themselves effectively. To begin with, they did not see the enemy: no one could have foreseen that the danger lay before them in their own land. Beyond this, from the first days of the colonialist-assisted revolution, the objectives of the simple Tutsis and of the Tutsi elite were not the same: while the former struggled to physically survive, the latter bargained for political survival. What resistance was organized by Tutsi leaders only resulted in further repression, in the form of revenge missions which took the lives of untold numbers of Tutsi peasants. For example, in 1963 a small number of Tutsis (not more than a hundred) from among those who escaped the massacres by fleeing to neighboring Burundi decided to attack Kigali:

> When they reached the Kanzenze Bridge… they were stopped by regular National Guard troops. Of course, these [Tutsi] were armed only with bows and spears. The Tutsis tried to fight against the Guard troops, who were by now well-trained soldiers with firearms.
> *Alexis Kagame*

On the hills far way from the capital, the enormous Hutu majority were already excited by the hate propaganda of their leaders; the provocative actions of high-ranking Tutsi traditionalists made the situation worse. When it became evident that up-country the Tutsi remained, in fact, at the mercy of people intent on becoming their executioners, simple Tutsi men started to organize a rudimentary system of self-defense. But on hills and in their round cattle-yards, these Tutsi giants were, for all their strength, far too vulnerable; they did not feel as though they were on a genuine field of battle. Tutsi traditions did not provide for fighting against neighbors or for killing children, the elderly or women. And it was absolutely inconceivable for a Tutsi to kill or maim someone's cow: cows are objects of love in the Tutsi world. In short, the "armed" Tutsis were not prepared to meet fire with fire outside the bounds of their culture.

I cannot speak to the abstract concept of historical righteousness. But I know one thing only too well: the year 1959 saw in Rwanda the beginning of a nightmare for the entire Tutsi ethnicity. Pastors, teachers, cattle-breeders and shepherds who knew no sin were trapped in their own homeland with nowhere to go. All that was left for them was to look silently upward for aid from above. They waited until the insanity ran its course. At some point the Tutsi survivors were finally able to return to their life on the land they had worked for centuries. But the Tutsis did not see real peace return to their homes again. Though the Assisted Ethnic Revolution came to an end in 1962, the gradual extermination of the Tutsi ethnicity continued.

And the greatest disasters were yet to come.

Chapter 7

Persecution

To the Tutsi had been attributed an Ethiopian, Nile, Hamite, even European or Tibetan origin. All that would nourish the ideological theories of genocide in 1994.
Jean-Luc Chavanieux

The revolutionary rejection of the feudal past was soon transformed into something else—an ideology of ethnic intolerance. Sporadic killings of Tutsis continued even after revolution and independence, while plunder and robbery up-country became daily occurrences. Tutsi houses went on burning in the hills for all to see; there were no more illusions. The former revolutionaries (who were the most active marauders) obtained the highest positions of authority. Tutsis of influence—former provincial and local authorities—were either killed, imprisoned, or obliged to go into hiding. The deposed king was threatened, and left Rwanda after being denied even the symbolic dignity and personal security. Thus began a new era in Rwandan history.

The Hutu-biased government started to apply racial criteria systematically in its internal policies. On identity documents, ethnicity—Hutu, Tutsi or Twa—was frankly specified. In a very practical sense, being Tutsi served as a barrier to children's educational development—in secondary school, let alone university. This was presented as merely the repayment of a historical debt, because before independence most intellectuals had been Tutsis. In a sense, the new policy reminded some of the 1933 law "against the overcrowding of German schools", which restricted the Jewish enrollment in German high schools to 1.5 percent of the student body. But the similarity did not end there.

The Nazis' implacable hatred of the Jews rested on their distorted worldview, which saw history as a racial struggle. They considered the Jews a race whose goal was world domination and who, therefore, were an obstruction to Aryan dominance.... They considered it their duty to eliminate the Jews, whom they regarded as a threat.

Such racial differences needed to be scientifically determined by anthropological data: apparently, Jewish heads should be more round than Aryan ones, even though this was mostly in theory. But many Germans were measured to absolve themselves of the "taint" of Jewish genes...
Simon Wiesenthal Museum of Tolerance

Documentary evidence as well as living human memory testifies that in Rwanda the extent of the racism was no less than this. A representative example: in the 1960's and 70's, Tutsi boys coming from distant provinces sought to secure, at any price, identity cards which would label them Hutu. Without these they could not enroll in any institution and study. But even with such cards in hand these Tutsis were not guaranteed success: their legs were long and their noses narrow, so the cards would not change their features. Apparently, Rwandan anthropologists were also ready to measure skulls, noses and legs in order to have a "physical basis" for their eccentric theories about the racial origins of Rwanda's inhabitants.

In the 1960's and 70's, the Republic of South Africa became the object of sharp criticism around the world because its government adopted a segregation policy—called apartheid— to keep the nation's whites and blacks in separate worlds while living in the same country. In Rwanda similar segregation— Hutu from Tutsis—did not trouble world opinion at all. Was this perhaps because the people of both ethnicities were pitch-black?

Expelled from public service and deprived of education, most Rwandan Tutsis returned to traditional cattle breeding.

Very few of the intellectuals from the *ancien régime* were able to continue working: most left, frustrated by the overt discrimination or fearing for their lives. Among those who stayed was Alexis Kagame, a prominent Tutsi linguist, historian and ethnographer, whose writing I have already quoted. I read his books, written during the 1960's and 70's—a period of terrible persecution of the Tutsis. I tried to find in them hidden references to anti-Tutsi discrimination. But I could not find any. The scholar wrote mostly about the past, but did not touch upon contemporary matters: this was obviously taboo. And observing this taboo may well have been a condition exacted for his personal safety.

In 1973 Rwanda once again saw a massive and well-organized massacre of Tutsis. In fact, this only represented a kind of historical punctuation mark: the ethnic slaughter had never entirely stopped before this and it did not cease afterward. Among our family legends there is the following story.

My maternal great-grandfather, by name Budenderi, had been well known as a warrior from the 1930's onward. He began regular patrols of his patrimony with guard dogs when colonial administrators first appeared on the outskirts of his *urugo*. His dogs announced the approach of undesirable strangers. Not heeding this warning, an unwelcome visitor could suddenly receive an arrow in his throat. Several times the colonial authorities investigated Budenderi and even imprisoned him, but in vain: released for lack of evidence, he continued to keep his land an island of independence. No one entered it without his permission or passed nearby without being detected. So when the first Tutsi massacre took place in the province of Gitarama during the revolution, Budenderi organized among his relatives and devoted servants a rota for round-the-clock guard duty. Always armed with bow and arrow, inseparable from his long pipe and vigilant dogs, Budenderi kept his plot of land unapproachable. Over all the years when the Tutsis were being persecuted, Hutu marauders could never threaten him. His family and servants kept on eating traditional food: meat cooked on a small fire for three days; green vegetables; sorghum pasta; home-made sorghum beer; milk. The enemy had to wait until 1994 to finally take over his land—but by that time old Budenderi had long since gone to his reward.

Chapter 8

Exile

There we wept, when we remembered Zion.
Psalm 137

Most of the Rwandan Tutsis who have survived to this day owe their very existence to exile. The exodus of the Tutsis from Rwanda started during the first days of the ethnic revolution. People fled, saving their lives but abandoning households and cattle. From one of my father's friends, David Ndaruhutse, I heard the following story.

In 1959 David was a child of no more than four: the only thing he remembered from that time was his name and the horrible scene of the slaughter of his parents, which he witnessed from behind banana trees. Only a few days prior to that, as the attacks on Tutsis had begun in the area, David's father had instructed his children: if the bad people come, everybody run across the border-river and hide there somewhere. And little David did just that, thanking God later that the river was only twenty yards wide and very shallow.

David was alone in the forest; not a single member of the family had ended up with him. He does not remember who found him and what happened next. But he spent the rest of his childhood in a refugee camp in Uganda, retaining from the past only his name—no parents, no relatives and no home. That refugee camp became his home: at the camp he attended a school and from there he went on to university. He used to return to the camp during vacations; he had nowhere else to go.

Some twenty-three years later he finally found his older sister. In fact, it was she who found him, because he hardly remembered the names of his family members, while she clearly did. All these years the sister, who had also fled to

Uganda, had been living in another refugee camp. Like him, she had thought herself the only survivor. Later David and his sister found some other family members, all living in different places and different countries.

This story is typical. At all events, after the colonial administration granted Rwanda independence and left the country in 1962, the new national authorities did not hide their intention of ridding the country of the remaining Tutsi presence.

Families and small groupings of Tutsis of all states and conditions (though mostly simple peasants) continued to cross the border in increasing numbers to seek asylum in neighboring Burundi, Uganda, or the Congo, whichever lay closer. Those who escaped death had nothing with which to start a new life in a strange country: their property had been burned and their cattle slaughtered. In exceptional cases some had been able to bring a pair of cows with them, but across the border no one provided pasture to feed the cattle. A few intellectuals with university diplomas could get jobs in exile; the overwhelming majority embarked on the miserable life of refugees, with no property and no rights. Almost none of the refugees sought to change their Rwandan nationality, even though the government of Rwanda did not recognize them any longer as citizens. Not only ethnic Tutsis went into exile, by the way. There were Hutu and Twa who were against the new authorities as well. Many who had refused to participate in the theft of Tutsi goods and property were threatened with death for their recalcitrance, and finally left. Abroad they shared the same destiny as the Tutsi refugees.

Years ago I read this report relating to another historical context, another people and another culture:

> From 1933 to 1939 concerted efforts were made by the Nazi party and agencies of the government to eliminate Jews from economic life... The stated objective of the Nazi regime was: Jewish emigration. In November 1938, following the assassination of a German diplomat in Paris by a young Jew,

all synagogues in Germany were set on fire, windows of Jewish shops were smashed, and thousands of Jews were arrested. This "Night of Broken Glass" was a signal to Jews in Germany and Austria to leave as soon as possible. Several hundred thousand people were able to seek asylum in other countries, but a similar number, including many who were old or poor, stayed to face an uncertain fate.
Raul Hilberg

The historical parallels with what was happening to my people arose by themselves, requiring no effort on my part to search them out. What was most striking about them, in any case, was not the similarities, great as they were; it was, rather, the simple realization that what had happened to us transpired long after Nazism in Europe had been identified, defeated and publicly condemned forever. The civilized world had already pronounced: "Never again!" What happened to the Tutsi people during the 1960's, 70's and 80's supposedly could not happen in the modern world! And yet as ethnic cleansing took place again, this time in a distant part of Africa, no one even noticed it. Belgium, the former colonial power, still claimed to be assisting Rwanda in its "peaceful" transition from feudalism to democracy.

My parents were among those who left their patrimony to seek asylum in neighboring countries. I grew up, together with my brother and sisters, among strange cultures, nations, languages and dialects. My principal memory of childhood is a feeling of alienation, a sense that we were not like other people; we were foreigners with no rights, a concept I could hardly grasp as a child—and yet instinctively I did. I knew that I was not at home: I was a newcomer, and an undesirable one, in someone else's land. I remember that in one place we lived I had to pass through a schoolyard in order to get to my home. Every time the pupils saw me they shouted: "Look at her long face! Next time you pass through here, we'll take a knife and reshape it for you!" I cried silently and began to dislike my own face—my own face! In the end I had to choose another way home.

There were many such incidents in our lives. My parents' only dream, and their one constant prayer, was to one day see Rwanda again—so beloved by them and now so far away. After many years this dream became a reality, but the price the family paid for it was high.

The first conscious memories I have of the great city of Kinshasa, where we lived for a period, are those one associates with a true megalopolis—all the imaginable and unimaginable crimes of a big city. Those aside, in comparing the countries which gave asylum to the Tutsis, the Congo was perhaps the friendliest. Most of the refugees who had formerly been up-countrymen could obtain land for cultivation in the Congo. Children took advantage of education in a Francophone environment. Some educated Rwandans even obtained relatively good jobs. My father was able to complete his studies, too. In the evening I often saw him listening to the radio. Our parents were afraid for our relatives still in Rwanda, where organized massacres of Tutsis had started again in 1973. Finally Mum and Dad decided to move as close to the Rwandan border as possible, to be able to assist relatives in case they needed to escape. The family went to Burundi.

In Burundi, father obtained a job as a teacher in a lycée in the capital Bujumbura. He taught courses in history, geography and ethics. As a pastor, he often preached at the Anglican Church in Bujumbura. I used to accompany him on Sundays, helping to carry his bag with robes and pastoral accessories. After nearly every service, people gathered around him for further discussion and his ministry continued for many more hours. In general, Tutsi communities in exile prayed long and fervently. In Burundi they made up the majority of the choirs in Catholic and Protestant churches. Perhaps this religious commitment was due to the extreme poverty and discrimination the Tutsis faced; they could find no solution.

I look to the mountains; where will my help come from?
My help will come from the Lord, who made heaven and
earth...
Psalm 121

When we lived in Bujumbura I left every morning for
school with my sister at 7:00 a.m. Passing near the big Catholic
Church, we always saw the Rwandan women who swept the
churchyard and watered the flowers. They did not earn money
for this; it was done as a tribute to God. I still hold this
memory of their silent devotion after so many years. A young
Tutsi woman, Anne Mukankusi, lived near us; she had five
children. Formally uneducated, she could nevertheless read
and write. She got up very early every morning, did all the
housework, prepared the food and fed her children, and then
went to church. She led the choir there for years; it was like her
job. Her husband did not like it, and sometimes beat his
beautiful wife because of it. But she used to say: here in exile I
am jobless; but when we go back to our country, God has
promised me a job and a nice house. We did not believe her,
taking what she said as a kind of optimistic humor.

Beyond the trials and hardships, however, it is also true
that these years represented a period of new self-identification:
for the first time in their history the Tutsis were seeking their
place among other nations.

Viewed from the personal side, exile is obviously suffering,
breakdown, even loss of identity. But it can also offer an
opportunity for self-reconstruction: far from one's own
country, exile can provide one a new look; facing another
culture and society can fertilize one with a new experience...
Jacques Seebacher

It is hard to convey the extent of the poverty in which
many refugees lived. More than once I noticed that our
neighbor lady, Mrs Peruth Mukamana, had nothing to cook—

but made a fire on the *imbabura* charcoal tin-oven and boiled a towel in a saucepan on it, as if it were food. She did not want to show her destitution, either to her neighbors or to her children—who often, after hours of waiting, went to bed hungry. When we could, we invited these children to share our dinner.

Our family was surely happier than many, and we were grateful to God for keeping us alive. Everyone loved my father, as he was a good and kind man. In Burundi I went to school like any other child; I could speak the local language fluently, since it was quite similar to our own. Perhaps it seems curious, but my personal relations with Burundian Hutus were always good. As children, we played together, told jokes, and returned home together in the evening. How can one explain this? Perhaps they knew that the Tutsis in Rwanda were also suffering as they themselves suffered: by that time, the Hutus in Burundi had been largely excluded from political life, just as the Tutsis had been in Rwanda.

Meanwhile, politics started to affect the family again— though we ourselves had done nothing to warrant this. First, my father lost his job as a teacher owing to a government edict which restrained pastors from working outside churches. It may be that this order was merely a pretext to cover the provision of a few additional working places. In any case, the Anglican Church in Bujumbura could not quite support its own pastors, let alone foreigners. By that time, tens of thousands of Rwandan Tutsis were living in Burundi, and the resources of the country were stretched thin.

Tension between local people and the refugees increased. Little by little, it became difficult for us refugee children to study. In the public schools, a mark for nationality stood in the class registry right after each pupil's name. In order to get access to secondary education, the first obstacle was the National School Competition Test. The passing score for Burundian children was about 50 percent, whereas for us foreigners it was 80 percent or more—so most of us could not pass. Many had to repeat the same class three, four, five, even six times! One could have very good marks during the year, but after taking the National Test still not find himself on the list of successful pupils. This was frustrating and awful. Non-nationals had practically no right even to claim their exam papers. Some tried to change their Rwandan names to Burundian, thus hoping to escape discrimination. It helped little. Only a few succeeded in getting into a secondary school, usually if their parents were able to pay the higher private college fees. But most refugee children's families did not even have the money necessary to pay the regular school fee. Our father prayed hard for us and made up practice tests for me and my younger sister to take at home. Eventually both of us succeeded in obtaining our secondary school diplomas.

It is saddening—but not hard to understand—that a huge proportion of the Rwandan Tutsi children abroad gave up school. Without education, of course, prospects were limited, particularly for girls. Some of the luckier ones were attractive enough to secure desirable marriages. Indeed, rumors of Rwandan feminine beauty still circulate around the world. Miss France of 2000, for example, is the daughter of a French father and of a Tutsi mother. Everywhere one can find Tutsi women married to well-known and prominent men: these women become Congolese, Burundians, Malians, Senegalese, French, Germans, Belgians, Italians... But in relation to the total number of refugees, such cases of fortunate marriage were the rarest of exceptions; many of my former classmates finished up as prostitutes in the streets of Bujumbura. And not only there: wherever you go in central Africa you will find these tall and beautiful girls, true black beauties, becoming prostitutes. That is only a part of the terrible price my people have paid for survival: to support their families, these young princesses were sometimes obliged to sell themselves for a mere handful of food...

Not only was financial need a constant problem, but the very status of refugee, and even the term itself, represented a difficult burden for the proud Tutsis to bear. One of my teachers at Bujumbura Saint-Esprit College, a professor of chemistry and a Rwandan Tutsi, was a highly regarded specialist and held a well-paid job; yet his Burundian pupils still called him by the nickname "Mr. HCR" (after the High Commission for Refugees), because both local children and their parents were convinced that every refugee went to the HCR headquarters to draw social assistance at the end of the month. In the Congo, the Tutsis were often nicknamed "Nilotiques", which signified "coming from the Nile", and also "made from nylon", because their thin and wiry physiques suggested they were people without much physical force. In Uganda, many Tutsis lived in densely-packed refugee camps. Children grew into adults, still having no legal address other than the refugee camp. Many there were killed mercilessly under the regime of President Obote, when organized massacres of Tutsi refugees became a rather regular event.

I cannot convey the beauty and wisdom of the elderly Tutsis, those old men and women refugees who were far from their homes. If you have not seen them, you cannot imagine their grace and politesse. Today I do not see a single Rwandan who resembles these noble souls! They were always very clean. The old women cared for their black hair assiduously, always keeping it in place. They usually wore traditional Tutsi dress. If you saw them passing, you would ask yourself how anyone could say that the Tutsis were poor. They always held that one day, although that day was unknown, all Rwandans in exile would go back to their own country. By that time, some Tutsis were already working in Europe and in America, many having adopted new nationalities—although they still considered themselves Rwandans.

In the late 1980's, a glimmer of hope appeared for the first time in many years. Beginning in 1987, a small newspaper, *Impuruza*, started to circulate among Tutsi refugees. At home I often saw our father reading it. A new generation was appearing, a generation of Tutsis like me: we had grown up abroad, never having seen our country with our own eyes. The editorials in this newspaper called upon the Tutsis to regain their rights.

The Tutsi diaspora started to think more and more of returning home. Having no more means to continue in exile, people started to apply to the Rwandan Government, and personally to the then President Habyarimana, to allow them to come back. These claims were usually rejected under the pretext that Rwanda's resources did not allow the country to accept foreign immigrants. A few refugees, as rare exceptions, did manage to return.

One day in 1990, I remember our father announcing that soon he might be able to go back to Rwanda: he had gotten a job as a pastor at the very same Presbyterian church where he had started out so many years ago! He knew quite well that for a Tutsi to return to Rwanda could mean putting his life in danger; but who can stop a man, now well into middle age, from returning to the green hills where he was born, and where his elderly parents were still alive? In spite of all the warnings, father decided he should go back—even if he had to leave his wife and children behind for a time. I remember one early morning, after sincere and ardent prayer, we saw our father off. We finally got a message from him after three long months—and we cried with joy. A few months after that he managed to come to visit us in Burundi for a short time, even though a journey by bus was for a Tutsi an extremely dangerous enterprise. When the day came for him to leave again, I remember Dad rising very early, perhaps 3:30 in the morning. My brother was accompanying him, and they told me to stay at home. I went outside to see him off. When he was already far away, I burst out sobbing: I had a feeling that I would never see him again.

It was around this time that Rwandan radio started to bring more and more alarming news. The word *"Twabamaze!"*, which means: "Tutsis are no more!" – became a common refrain on the airwaves from official Rwandan radio stations.

> RTLM, Radio Rwanda, Kangura – the propaganda of these
> hate-radio stations openly sought to transform a social
> consciousness into an ethnic and racial one: the long-legged
> ones "should be shortened" and "those with narrow noses"
> [dealt with]...
> *Jean-Luc Chavanieux*

We also listened to these broadcasts. The extent of the official hatred of the Tutsis was so strong that radio announcers often called us *inyenzi*, cockroaches. This was not mere rhetoric; after all, preparing a people to wipe out another people takes a certain amount of effort. A first step is to convince the former that killing the latter, though they seem human, is actually like killing a cockroach.

Nearly all of us refugees had at least a few family members in Rwanda, and our hearts were breaking. The arrest and jailing of Tutsis became more and more frequent, and included those who had never left the country and had remained Rwandan citizens. It was impossible not to be concerned about what was going to happen to them, surrounded as they were by hostile neighbors and openly mistreated by the authorities. Only high-ranking officials at the UN headquarters needed confidential reports by experts to determine what was at hand. None of us, the simple people living in the region, needed such expertise: reading the local newspapers and listening to what was openly said on the radio was entirely sufficient. We sensed the stench of the genocide in the air.

In 1990 a group of courageous young Tutsis, people who had grown up in refugee camps in Uganda, started to organize an armed force on the Rwandan border. Fred Rwigema, Paul Kagame and others were among this group. After some time they were able to take control of a forested area in the northern Rwandan provinces, establishing their military bases there. Under the name of the Rwandan Patriotic Front (RPF), they declared themselves a political force and started to negotiate with the central Rwandan government over the question of legally returning to the country.

The RPF soon emerged as the single real opposition force against the Rwandan totalitarian regime. As such it attracted to its ranks not only Tutsis, but also many exiled Hutu politicians. The ruling regime was, clearly, not eager to advance the opposition's political agenda; and the less progress the negotiations made, the greater was the appeal of force as an alternative. During those years I remember that many of my friends, young Tutsi boys from the Congo and Burundi, volunteered to join others at the front to fight for the freedom of Rwanda. Some even left just before graduation from the university—such was the urgency of the moment.

My older brother, too, gave up his studies at the university and started working to raise money for the front. He labored whenever and wherever possible; he was always away somewhere, and often we did not hear from him for weeks. In fact, all the Tutsis we knew started to contribute money, clothes and whatever else they could for the front. Students also contributed a part of their scholarship money. For example, out of my monthly scholarship of some 15,000 Burundian Francs (roughly US$60), which I received at the University of Burundi, I contributed one third to the needs of the front. All my Rwandan Tutsi fellow-students did the same. We tried to survive on the remainder, knowing that up there at the front our brothers were offering far more than this—their very lives. They were fighting against the regular troops of the ruling Rwandan regime; and this regime was being supported militarily by various European powers, in particular by France, which considered the Rwandan leader Juvenal Habyarimana a favorite partner.

In the meantime, some progress was (apparently) achieved with the participation of the UN. An agreement between the ruling Rwandan regime and the RPF was signed at Arusha, Tanzania, in 1993. This agreement provided for a sharing of power among the various political protagonists, and for Tutsi refugees it seemed to offer some reason to hope for a return home. Perhaps for the first time history provided an opportunity for Rwandans to gradually bring under control the consequences of a bizarre, colonially-led decolonization. But the chance was missed. The hard-line Hutu nationalists surrounding Rwandan President Habyarimana instinctively feared the return of the Tutsis—and they carried the day. The agreement, once a beacon of hope, was not implemented. In fact it was disavowed altogether by the ruling regime. Everyone understood what that meant: negotiations would now give way to military force.

I watched this entire chain of events from Burundian side of the border. In 1993, a time of a terrible ethnic tension descended on Burundi itself. Apparently this fact had a deleterious effect on the Rwandan peace process, because fear is a bad adviser to negotiators—and Burundi served as a rather negative example.

In Burundi, Tutsi leaders had held power since 1972. In 1993, for the first time, a Tutsi president had given up supreme power to a new Hutu leader; but instead of resolving the existing ethnic tensions by progressive means, the new Burundian government chose the way of unleashing uncontrolled Hutu nationalism and launching repression against the Tutsis.

I witnessed how things went from bad to worse for Tutsi in Burundi. Before the elections, the Hutu opposition managed to clandestinely reach the remotest area of the country with frank ethnically-biased appeals. Long before the Election Day, my Hutu friends told me: be prepared to leave. They told how the team of the new leader had promised Burundian Hutus the property of the Tutsis after the victory. I have heard myself in one of the meetings as one Hutu orator pointed to the finest houses, situated on the Kiriri hill of the Capital (mostly Tutsi had lived there): "Why should they live up there, and you down here? They should go down, and you should go up!" In other electoral meeting, the Hutu female activist addressed to the multitude of women: "Those eating potatoes are no better than you eating manioc!" For those who live in Burundi it was clear what she meant; she meant Tutsis and Hutus...

At the same time, the press releases prepared by the opposition leader for foreign diplomats were perfectly politically correct. On the radio and in newspapers, the official rhetoric also was: no longer ethnic division! The nation was allegedly united as never before around the acting President, who was portrayed as the best representative of the consolidated people. Immense crowds of cherishing Hutu peasants awaited the Presidential cortège on every hill he choose to go. Hutu activists instructed them: show as much devotion as you can; but you would know how to vote on the Election Day. The result was: an overwhelming victory of the Hutu opposition. The percentage of ballots for Tutsi and Hutu candidate in each community exactly matched their ethnic composition...

I was not far from our home in Bujumbura when it was announced that the Hutu leader had won the elections in Burundi. Immediately after this I heard great and joyful shouting in the streets: the Hutus were running about crying *"Inkoko yabitse!"*, "Our hour has come!" In the eyes of the Tutsis one could read only fear: what would happen to us? Everyone remembered the massacres of the Tutsis in Rwanda after they had lost political power there. The next day I went to the university campus as usual; there I found Tutsi students demoralized and desperate. I heard one Burundian say "Now we are about to become refugees in our own country..." And indeed, the worst-case scenario started to play itself out in Burundi over the next few months.

After successful elections and transition of the power, the Hutus, from servant boys on up, reasonably expected the promises to be fulfilled. I was told about one Hutu servant who announced to his Tutsi boss: "Why not give me the keys to the house and the car now? You will have to leave soon anyway..." Within two months the newly elected leader began to change everything and everyone in public service, management and government. In the end, after he announced the firing of a group of high-ranking Tutsi military officers, the period of peaceful transition of power came to an end. A military coup was carried out, and the new leader was summarily executed. This triggered a true ethnic war in Burundi. Hutu rebels started attacking and killing Tutsis whenever and wherever possible, generally at night; the army organized and led revenge operations. The rebels, after fighting at night, would return in the morning to their wives and children—rendering them vulnerable as targets of revenge missions.

For us Rwandan Tutsis, who had fled to Burundi to escape death, things had changed catastrophically: once again we became the subject of a campaign of enraged ethnic cleansing—but this time in a country where we had no interests, no possessions, and no influence whatever.

The mere fact that we were Tutsis was apparently enough to warrant our extermination. Prior to this, we had lived in Bujumbura together, Tutsis and Hutus sharing the same quarters—with no distinctions among us. But after October 1993, night assaults with guns, grenades, knives and stones became part of everyday life. Very soon our quarters in Bujumbura became monoethnic, as all the Tutsis moved towards the areas where they could stay close together. Every day the specter of imminent and cruel death approached our home. Our remaining men and youngsters started patrolling the streets at night to protect us from Hutu extremists. But now and then, grenade explosions announced that the enemy had penetrated into the area. Every morning we could see how the toll of destroyed houses had grown overnight. Finally we started to sleep outside for fear the assassins would break in at night. Now we children knew the same experience our mother had been through as a young girl in Rwanda after the ethnic revolution. In the daytime, schools were mostly empty; but the university, incongruously, was still operating. In the morning, on my way to the campus, I usually saw several dead bodies lying on both sides of the highway.

Burundian Hutu students from our university suddenly started to disappear, most likely having joined the rebel forces. At least once at night I heard the voice of a boy across the fence, saying to another: "Don't touch that house, these are my friends…" It may have been one of my former classmates. As for the Burundian Tutsis, they began to express a new sympathy for us, the Rwandan Tutsi refugees, feeling that soon they themselves might have to seek asylum.

In Rwanda by that time the Hutus had split in two camps—moderates and the hard-liners. While the first still recognized the necessity of dealing politically deal with the Tutsis, the others set about a plan long in the making: to exterminate all the Tutsis; to be done with them forever, so that no more Tutsi seed would survive in the Rwandan hills… The Rwandan Patriotic Front, by that time holding the northern provinces of Rwanda, became the only hope for Tutsis—those both within and outside Rwanda.

My extended family was spread about: my father preached peace at the Presbyterian church in Kigali; many relatives were in Gitarama and still other Rwandan provinces; many others were outside Rwanda in exile like us. None of us, anywhere, knew what lay ahead. But those who had prepared the Rwandan final solution had already primed the explosives. Only a single spark was needed to blow up our ancient and beautiful land.

That spark was not long in coming.

Chapter 9

Genocide

That nice summer in 1994, an exceptional event took place in Rwanda, sir. In that distant Africa, which had seemed so wild to us, the 20th century came tumbling down without so much as a shout. It happened in the form of genocide, which means: a massive extermination organized by a state in an industrial way.
Patrick de Saint-Exupéry, L'inavouable. La France au Rwanda.

The events which transpired in Rwanda from April through June of 1994 are commonly called the Rwandan genocide. As a final homage to those who can no longer speak for themselves, I will call these events by their proper name: the Tutsi genocide in Rwanda.

Each human being is unique, and his death means an end to a unique universe. Therefore there can be no such thing as a history of human death: each one will forever remain individual. Nevertheless, genocide as a phenomenon has its own grim history. In Biblical times, it was not unusual to kill everyone in a conquered city, down to "the one urinating on the wall." In the sixteenth century, St. Bartholomew's Night became a synonym for massacre on religious grounds. In the beginning of the twentieth century, masses of Armenians were killed by the Turks simply because they were Armenians (and not because they were Christians). Finally, the German Nazis invented the entire ideology of the holocaust and began a methodical and "rational" extermination of the Jews, who before that had suffered terrible pogroms in Russia, and before that persecution in Spain... In this sad, inhuman context, what was the distinctive feature of the Rwandan tragedy? What made it special? It was indeed special.

None of the previous genocides needed to be camouflaged as something else. But the Tutsi genocide in Rwanda for a time existed under the mask of spontaneous ethnic violence. This term was evidently enough to allay the fears of most officials at the United Nations headquarters. It allowed the Rwandan regime to profit from significant and continuous Western military assistance, especially from France, under the pretext of the need to maintain public order.

France! The cradle of European democracy and ultimate hope for so many of the world's oppressed! How could it come to pass that the French state continued to help a clearly corrupt and manifestly evil African client state? The French supplied the Habyarimana regime with arms, ammunition and advisors. This support continued in spite of what eyewitnesses began to report regularly and in no uncertain terms: what was underway was no longer an "ethnic conflict"! Military units and organized militias, it was reported, were hunting down the Tutsi civilian population and exterminating them. Only when the mass killings became so overt that blood started to engulf the Rwandan rivers did France finally cease its support of the criminal regime. By that time it was too late to prevent the death of 95 percent of the Tutsi population of the country.

> A few steps away stood an officer of our elite unit GIGN. He stood downcast, his legs rigid, and he seemed to be absent. We encircled him, sir, many of us. We thought he had broken down, which would be understandable. But he was a soldier and a warrior. That was not the problem. The problem was something else, something much more serious. He had just realized, just understood, just taken into account what had happened. He turned to us and said: "Last year I trained the Rwandan Presidential guards." His eyes were wild. He was lost. The past illuminated the present. He had trained masse murderers, the perpetrators of genocide. This was frightening.
> *Patrick de Saint-Exupéry*: L'inavouable. La France au Rwanda.

To this day great effort continues to be expended, both in Rwanda and abroad, to shift the accents when speaking of the bloody drama of 1994. There are people who say, "Yes, we admit it was terrible; yes, we recognize the incredible number of victims among the Tutsi civilians. But it was a war, so the casualties were unavoidable. Also, lest we forget, many people were lost on both sides. And in the end, how long can one keep talking about this ethnic conflict? Both Hutu and Tutsis were implicated; for the future of the nation, should we not pardon each other now and start building a new Rwanda?"

I am not a politician or a diplomat. In such excuses I clearly hear the desperate and faltering speech of a trapped criminal: having no way to deny the truth, he tries at least to turn things around, to deflect attention away from his guilt. Surely no one wants more blood: enough is enough, for all the past and future generations. But while we have to forgive what happened, there is no way to forgive what is denied. I will continue my story as we Tutsi have lived it.

April 7, 1994—none of us will ever forget that day. That morning an unprecedented slaughter began in Rwanda. The night before an airplane was shot down from the sky above Kigali. An unknown but undoubtedly professional hand had launched a missile at it. Not only did that missile target the president of Rwandan regime, accompanied by his Burundian counterpart, but it also targeted the lives of millions of Rwandans.

The massacre did not start impulsively or spontaneously; all evidence indicates that the plane crash was in fact a long-awaited signal. Its message was: "Stop negotiations with the Tutsis; no more UN observers; enough playing games! Begin what has been on the agenda for a long time: the Final Solution! Have done with the entire long-legged race, these cockroaches, before they turn up once again in our ministerial offices!" The signal was received. The ruling regime had sufficient resources for the task: a trained army and military police; elite units of the presidential guards; a highly efficient network of provincial administrators; and enormous numbers of local militias. The former president had been afraid to use these resources effectively, preferring endless negotiations. Now, when the president was no longer an obstacle, nothing could stop this assembled might from doing what it had been designed to do—exterminate the Tutsis. And hundreds of thousands of Rwandan Tutsis lost their lives during the next three months.

People all around the world continue to ask themselves: how on earth could such a thing happen—at the end of twentieth century, in a member-country of the United Nations and under the mandate of the UN Blue Berets? Perhaps the best way to understand this is to turn to the recently published memoirs of Lieutenant-General Roméo Dallaire, the Commander-in-Chief of the UN Assistance Mission for Rwanda (UNAMIR) at the time:

> Shortly after the Rwandan President's airplane was shot down over the capital on April 6th, 1994...I called New York. It was midnight in Kigali, and about 15:00 in New York. I said: if we had a chance to put Rwanda back on the Arusha path, we must not let the opportunity slip away. Otherwise we would again be surrendering the initiative to the extremists and become nothing more than witnesses to a human catastrophe. The answer came back loud and clear: I was not to take sides, and it was up to the Rwandans to sort things out themselves... They told me not to risk UNAMIR troops, to help with the security of all UN civilians and dependants, to keep in close touch with the expatriate and diplomatic communities and to update my withdrawal plan and be ready to implement it. I hung up feeling angry, empty and in a state of moral and ethical conflict.
> *Roméo Dallaire,* Shake Hands with the Devil: The Failure of Humanity in Rwanda

More than ten years after these events one finds the following comment from an internet columnist, which needs no commentary:

The Rwandan genocide remains one of the gloomiest episodes in

United Nations history and a source of embarrassment for Secretary-General Kofi Annan, the head of the Department for Peacekeeping Operations (DPKO) at that time. The United Nations revealed its incapacity to control the events in spite of appeals for aid coming from Kigali.
Yahoo Actualité, 7 June 2004

On September 11, 2001, in New York City, more than two thousand innocent people perished within a few minutes. It is hard for us to comprehend such a large number of victims in such a small period. But we have to make the effort in order to do justice to the tragedy. In Rwanda, **four times as many people were murdered each day, and this process went on for a long hundred days**...

I was not in Rwanda at that time. If I had been it is unlikely that I would be here now to write these lines. My father and many of my relatives were there. From abroad we helplessly waited for any news from them, but we had no illusions as to what was happening. Over an area of 26,000 square kilometers the devil, suddenly set free, was running wantonly. There was no one to stop him and almost no one to bear witness. As the first murders among expatriates were reported, the several hundred representatives of the international community were evacuated in helicopters and armored cars. Tutsi men, women and children remained alone with those who sought their souls. Though everyone had anticipated a wave of killings, no one had expected the rapidity and level of organization that it started with. On April 7, armed military appeared in virtually all the important Tutsi houses in Kigali and executed their inhabitants on the spot. The same was done to a few Hutu politicians, those who were commonly called "moderates".

Between April and July 1994, eight hundred thousand to a million men, women and children were assassinated. Killing so many people must have been a difficult job. The presidential guards and regular military units could not manage it on their own; they needed the help of the local militias and Interahamwe—units of young extremists, created long in advance for this purpose. The guards and military units provided these forces with machetes, grenades, wood saws and kerosene...

From the first day of the genocide, the telephone lines in Kigali were cut down; but for some reason mobile phones were still working. On the evening of April 7 my sister managed to make a call from Bujumbura to my uncle's mobile number. The uncle related that he and his family were trying to hide somewhere in the house, because there was no more chance to get outside and escape that way. Here and there he could hear the cries of terrified people; many houses were being set on fire; armed militia men and Interahamwe were running around. The next morning my sister called again, but there was no more answer from the phone. The whole family had been savagely killed that night.

A few brave Hutu tried to hide Tutsis; but these were not many, since the risk of sharing the Tutsis' fate was real. Even if you had a Hutu family friend, this friendship could not be expected to endure through these days. Tutsis who tried to ask friends for shelter were usually sent away. Some were reported to local authorities which meant to be sentenced to death.

In the Gikondo quarter of Kigali, one can see to this day an ordinary African house encircled by a fence: this house became grimly famous in the hardest days of April 1994. Among the frightened and terrified Tutsis of the quarter, the rumor spread that some people could gain asylum in that house, which belonged to a respected Hutu landlord. Later it was revealed what actually happened there: the Interahamwe had set a trap: they stayed inside, made the owner welcome the asylum-seekers, and then killed them on the spot once they entered the house. Over the course of three nights the house became full of dead bodies, until the stench became unbearable to the executioners themselves.

> Although the entire German population was not in agreement with Hitler's persecution of the Jews, there is no evidence of any large-scale protest regarding their treatment. There were

Germans … who aided Jews to escape and to hide, but their number was very small.
Simon Wiesenthal Museum of Tolerance

Over the next few days, the whole of Rwanda was set on fire. Up-country, everybody knows everybody—so no lists were needed to identify Tutsi families. Hostages in their own homes, the Tutsis were surrounded by armed militia led not only by hate groups, but also by the local authorities. Thousands of people with nowhere to hide ran away to hospitals, schools, stadiums. No matter where they went, they found no protection from death. Their lives were worth no more than the effort needed to raise a dull machete or toss a lighted match…

At first nobody quite knew the real extent of the tragedy. We listened to the Rwandan government radio station Mille Collines. Day and night on that official station extremists encouraged soldiers, militiamen and simple peasants, in the Rwandan language, to kill: "Kill as many Tutsis as you can, let none of them escape!" Reports from Rwanda by Radio France International were not ethnically biased, but it made these reports even more frightening: they were simply true…. And foreign television coverage showed the swollen Nyabarongo river, where it leaves Rwanda. We saw the river filled with dead bodies. The bodies floated down, day by day and week by week, all the way to Lake Victoria.

The devil first confuses human beings before taking control of them. In those awful days, Christians no longer remembered God; next to the altar there was no longer any refuge. Hundreds of churches all across the country were turned into slaughterhouses for Tutsis who had hoped to escape death in them. The murderers did not hesitate to kill in churches. Indeed, among the killers were priests and nuns: many leaders of churches, both Catholic and Protestant, made a distinction among their Christian followers on ethnic grounds. Not all Hutu clergy participated in the "final solution" in person; some simply allowed militia members to enter churches where Tutsis were gathered around the altar. Members of the militias who belonged to the Seventh-day Adventists stopped killing on Saturdays, only to start again the next morning.

Most Hutu peasants were afraid they themselves would be killed if they refused to participate in the killing of the Tutsis. Hutu men having Tutsi wives readily delivered them to squads of killers to be violated and then murdered. Hutu women married to Tutsi men likewise acquiesced in the killing of their husbands and children, as the latter were also Tutsi by birth. Because of the common belief that Tutsi blood would prevail in the offspring, any child of a mixed marriage was considered Tutsi. It was like mass psychosis or mass drunkenness. Surely, a large draft of superstitious fear was mixed into this poisonous alcohol as well; along with the Tutsis, the killers slaughtered their cattle and even their cats! Yes, cats have always been associated with Tutsis in Rwandan poetic tradition: these gracious and supple animals have narrow noses and a fondness for milk. All this was far too reminiscent of Tutsis for the murderers to let cats remain alive...

Our mind refuses to believe. But a human being in these circumstances is no longer subject to common judgment. Only few voluntarily accept to die along with their family members. What commonly happened in my country: members of ethnically mixed families often bought their own lives by reporting their Tutsi relatives to the executors. And the executors were drunk by blood. They wanted more than a simple betrayal: they wanted a proof of loyalty from their Hutu fellows. A slight hesitation or lack of enthusiasm to participate in the "Final Solution" signified immediate and cruel death. About 50 000 Hutus were killed these days only for showing reluctance to participate in killings. Obviously, not all of the rest had opted for this fate. Many others, not given other chance to survive but to kill, would often do it in view of imminent death.

Man was turned into a killing machine. They managed to transform an entire people—men, women and children—into murderers...They ordered a man to kill and he did it...
Patrick de Saint-Exupery, L'inavouable. La France au Rwanda.

Such was the "Final Solution" *à la rwandaise*. In full accordance with the officially propagated policy of Rwanda, genetic inheritance constituted a sufficient criterion for execution. An identity card could be altered; but the physical appearance of a person is less easily changed. A Tutsi usually looks like a Tutsi—and this simple fact brought death to hundreds of thousands. The apparent goal of the campaign was a complete genetic cleansing.

Our brothers in the Rwandan Patriotic Front made every effort to advance from the north in time to save the people. But it was too late. The closer the fighting got, the greater was the danger to those civilian Tutsis who still remained alive. The criminal regime was about to collapse, and everyone understood this. Yet the closer this hour approached, the more efforts were made by the leaders not to let any Tutsi escape. During those last days of genocide, for a Tutsi to be merely killed was regarded as a favor. Death was rendered unspeakably. Tutsi infants were smashed against walls. Children and the elderly were forced head down into latrine holes and held there until they suffocated in feces. At first women and girls had simply been raped (to cries of "Let us first taste how these Tutsi women are!"). As the insanity reached its peak, thousands of Tutsi women and girls were violated in front of their children, husbands and parents, then killed by piercing: sharp wooden sticks were run through them, skewering them through the genitalia and out the throat...

If you looked, you could see the evidence, even in the whitened skeleton. The legs bent and apart. Broken bottles, a rough branch, even a knife between them...Some male corpses had their genitals cut off, but many women and young girls had their breasts chopped off and their genitals crudely cut apart. They died in a position of vulnerability, flat on their backs, with their legs bent and knees wide apart.

L.Gen. Roméo Dallaire: Shake Hands with the Devil

A handful of these violated Tutsi women managed to survive. Perhaps those who raped them hoped that soon they would infect many RPF soldiers: remaining alive, they surely had become carriers of HIV/AIDS. Nearly all of these poor victims have by now ended their days after terrible suffering and in frightening poverty.

During these three endless months we had no news from the father. We lost hope, because we knew that had he somehow remained alive, he would have managed to send us a sign by now. One night in June, I saw him in a dream at the head of a procession. All were dressed in white pastoral robes, walking at the side of a large meadow, like a football field, and singing "Hallelujah!" When I awoke that morning, I knew my father had gone to Glory. So when the news finally came, we were partly prepared. My older sister traveled closer to the Rwandan border, where the few Tutsis who had escaped death were gathered in camps. She hoped to find our father, or at least to find someone who knew of him. A woman there told her that we should not look for him any longer. Only when the armed forces of the Rwandan Patriotic Front took control of Kigali did we learn what had actually happened to our dad.

During the first days of the massacres, my father and four other pastors came to the Presbyterian Church—which is where all of them were captured. Some pastors had their children with them. There is evidence that some Hutu clergymen belonging to the same church assisted in the arrest. Reportedly, the Tutsi pastors were first told that they would be taken from the church to a more secure place in Gitarama.

The soldiers were at first hesitant: they did not dare kill so many servants of God all at once. So instead, they locked them in a former seminary building, hoping they would die there from hunger. But the people remained alive for a long time, and the guards became frightened. One day militiamen brought in eighteen more prisoners: these were Tutsi boys and girls from different Christian families (children who had been hidden by a Hutu Christian in his home until they were finally found). The next day, all the prisoners together—children and adults, not excluding the Hutu who had hidden the children— were savagely killed. Before killing the pastors, the murderers first took away their pastoral robes. But even naked and abused, the noble prisoners continued to pray until the very end. This happened in Taba, Gitarama prefecture, some 40 kilometers from Kigali. Local countrymen later showed us the mass grave the victims were buried in. This place is now a commemorated site.

Most of my relatives perished in Rwanda during those days. The first was my father's father, a retired pastor from Kibuye, and his wife, my grandmother. As I think of them, I see the small town where the couple had lived and preached their whole life. I cannot escape the feeling that among those who killed them may have been people who were baptized by my grandfather. From dad's side, I lost all my uncles, and all their children. From my mother's side, all her sisters, all her brothers and all her nieces perished. There is still a plot of land which belongs to my mother's family. But there is no one to live on it any more. Only an old cadastral record remains to bear witness to the names of all the former owners.

Those who survived did so only by miracles. Many of these miraculous stories are told when Tutsi families come together. For example, one of my distant relatives, whose wife and six children were all killed, was hidden for three months by an old Hutu woman whom he had known to be a good soul. This good lady lived up-country in a very poor house, which no one could suspect as a refuge; she herself was struggling for survival. The Hutu woman hid her guest in a straw roof; and he stayed inside that roof virtually all that time. At night the old woman brought him whatever she could provide, sometimes just water. He was afraid to come down even to wash or change clothes: the roof was for him everything, even a toilet. When it rained, he stayed in the water; when insects attacked him, he could not move; when malaria hit him, he could not get a Chloroquine tablet. How long can a human being keep up such a life? Eventually, he decided to die there, and one day he asked the lady not to bring him food any longer. And he would have died had he stayed there even a few more days. But the regime finally collapsed, and this distant relative of mine survived. As I was writing this, another person's testimony came to mind.

> I was a little girl then. The only people that knew my name were my parents. My father brought me into the house, and that was the last time I ever saw my father. I was hidden there for two years; I was not allowed to go outside because I did not belong to the family, and the woman who hid me sacrificed a lot to take me. Because had the Nazis discovered she was hiding a Jew—whether it was a little girl or an adult did not matter—they would have killed her on the spot. And me as well, of course.
>
> *Jeannine Burk*: Holocaust Survivors

One may find oneself asking, after all this, whether it is still worth living in such a world. But consider: the world is probably no better or worse now than it always has been. The old lady who hid my relative was a Hutu and not a German, but both did what they did—saved a life at the risk of their own—simply because they were human beings with a human heart: which, I am convinced, remains the same.

Was there any resistance from the Tutsis? There are not many examples. By 1994, a second generation of Tutsis had grown up in remote rural areas, marginalized and deprived of all social opportunities. None of the Tutsi boys had served in the army since 1959, so most had never seen modern weapons. But the main reason that there was so little resistance was that like all peasants, the rural Tutsis were accustomed to obeying the authorities: they simply could not imagine that they had been sentenced to extermination by these officials. So they came together at stadiums, churches or in hospitals, thinking they would be under the protection of the local administrations in these public places. They knew that in the past the murderers had come at night. They could not think that this time the masks would be lifted and the killing would take place in broad daylight. No one could have thought that this time the murderers would be led by the same administration which was supposed to protect the population.

It is also true to a certain extent that the massive Tutsi extermination became possible because the Tutsi people had confidence in an international presence. Even in very faraway locations they were accustomed to seeing a certain contingent of white people: representatives of churches, non-governmental organizations and, at the head of it all, the impressive blue UN flags. These flags gave the illusion that there was a real and effective UN presence in the country, while in fact the contingent had no mandate and was even forbidden to intervene. In any case, the visible international presence gave people hope that help would come; but it never did.

Nevertheless, even amidst wild hope and terrible desperation, there were Tutsis who clearly remained the descendants of the great warriors remembered in Africa to this day. One sees this in the story of the defenders of Bisesero, a dry hill situated in Kibuye prefecture, in the west of Rwanda. About 50,000 Tutsis, men, women, and children, fled there from surrounding villages hoping to escape death until some sort of help arrived. But there was no help; food and water were running out, and militia men, Interahamwe and soldiers were climbing closer up the hill with their guns, machetes and grenades. The encircled defenders took stones and threw them at the attackers, forcing them to withdraw; this desperate defense went on more than two months, until there were no more stones. The people on the hill became weaker and weaker with no food and only rainwater to drink. Everyone understood that the end was near. One day, as the enemy tried to advance, the entire remaining population on the hill, at the leader's signal, charged down and attacked the enemy with their hands in a final effort to escape death. Only a handful of the nearly fifty thousand people remained alive. The others chose to die on the battlefield, as this has always been considered an honor for a Tutsi.

The Tutsi genocide started in 1959, thirty five years before the explosion of April 1994; and unfortunately this genocide did not end in July 1994, when the RPF took full military control of the territory of Rwanda. The process of physical extermination of this minority people is going on even now: from time to time the news agencies report mass killings in remote Tutsi communities close to the Congolese border. But the worst, we hope and pray, has passed. The three spring months of 1994 will remain the nadir of our history—the point at which the very existence of Tutsis was uncertain.

In 1994, the Tutsis paid the highest possible price for their survival: hundreds of thousands of their sons and daughters. Is there another ethnic group in modern history which could suffer such irreplaceable losses and still maintain its identity? Most would probably disappear, their names lost to human posterity.

The Tutsi ethnicity survived.

Chapter 10

Back on Rwandan Hills

Imana yirirwa ahandi igataha i Rwanda (God passes the day abroad but at night He comes back to Rwanda).
Ancient proverb

The hot African sun, the lovely breeze and the wonderfully refreshing rains which fall in Rwanda at the beginning of every September produced a rather unexpected phenomenon in the fall of 1994. Only a few months after the slaughter, the omnipresent putrid stench of rotted flesh had almost completely disappeared. Unbelievably, it was gone. The air returned to its customary sweet and clean state, redolent only of unpolluted nature. The heavy odor of burned-out households turned little by little to the pleasant smell of the charcoal fires on which the women of Rwanda have prepared the evening meal for ages. Only the ugly litter of war—the carcasses of cars, the trenches, the craters and bombed-out buildings—remained as vivid reminders of the recent catastrophe. But the sky was as blue and sunsets as magnificent as they had always been. Nature was the first to heal from the war. It took much longer for the people to do so.

Be glad of life because it gives you the chance to love, and to work, and to play, and to look up at the stars...
Henry Van Dyke

On July 17, 1994, the entire territory of Rwanda was under the control of the Rwandan Patriotic Front, which finally stopped the organized extermination of the Tutsis. Most of the RPF soldiers had been born in exile. They were the sons of Rwandans who had left their homes many years before. So these soldiers liberated their ancestral homeland, which they saw for the first time in their lives. By that time, the Tutsis inside the country—those who had not been able to escape across state borders—were pitifully few. The corpses of the rest were stockpiled by the hundreds of thousands in shallow graves. Many thousands more still needed burial. No less than forty thousand decomposed bodies were found in Lake Victoria alone.

Those simple Hutus who had been in the militias—who murdered people, voluntarily or under compulsion, throughout the months of national psychosis—now returned to their normal occupations. They started using their agriculture tools as such implements are intended—to sow and gather crops—instead of as weapons. Inevitably, murderers now had occasion to meet, as life returned to sane dimensions, their former intended victims—people they had tried but not managed to kill. They were now condemned to live with one another.

The survivors of the genocide numbered only a handful, and they were in horrendous condition. Naturally thin in body type, the surviving Tutsis, after long weeks with no food, looked more like phantoms than human beings. Deep purulent wounds covered their once beautiful bodies. Terrifying machete cuts on their heads clearly showed the way in which some had escaped death: their executioners had thought they could not survive such wounds. Some managed to crawl away at night from beneath piles of dead bodies. Some hid for months in the bush with no access to any hygienic, let alone medical facilities; flies and worms had infested their wounds, producing a disgusting odor. These people were almost across the line which separates the living and the dead. Then one day they witnessed a miracle: young fighters came to bring them back to life. These soldiers showed kindness and affection towards their brothers. They carried the wounded who could not move any longer in their arms, no matter how ugly the wounds or how badly they smelled. The soldiers shared with them whatever food they could find in the ravaged countryside.

At this point most of the Rwandan Tutsi population which remained alive were outside the borders of Rwanda. A few had fled recently, escaping death by crossing the border within the last three months. Most had left the country as children or had been born abroad, like me. All of us started to look for a way to return. Our first thought, of course, was to find any family members who might possibly have survived. There were not many who did.

> Nothing would ever replace a lost companion... Nothing is worth the treasure of so many common memories; of the bad hours of life spent together, of so many quarrels, reconciliations, movements of the heart...
> *Antoine de Saint-Exupéry*: Terre des Hommes

The Tutsis began to arrive in Rwanda in large numbers almost immediately after the war was over. Their longing to finally become citizens in their own right was so strong that crowds overwhelmed the border checkpoints. Together with the Tutsis, the Hutus who had shared the destiny of the refugees were also returning. Families which had stayed abroad for decades sought urgently to sell their belongings, regardless of price, just to be able to see the country they had so long dreamt of. It was a time of fresh hope, when the whole nightmare seemed consigned to the past forever. An incredible spirit of brotherhood reigned among the former refugees. People from different countries, people separated for years, people who had lost so many loved ones—all of them helped and consoled one another, sharing bread, shelter and all their possessions.

Rwandan Tutsis who had lived in Burundi for many years were especially eager to return to Rwanda: the Burundian ethnic war that had begun in 1993 made the risk of being killed in Burundi quite real. These people said: It would be such a terrible shame to perish here now, when our own country finally awaits us. I saw my countrymen in Bujumbura urgently selling everything they owned for whatever they could get. What a joy it was to see them, left and right, packing their belongings. Families left in rented trucks, buses, and vans; they set off in rain or in good weather, without even knowing exactly where they were going—they simply knew they were returning to Rwanda. Some came back from Rwanda briefly to sell the rest of their belongings or businesses. What stories they told us about the homeland! It was beautiful, they said, except that there was still no running water or electricity, everything having been destroyed in the war. Also there were too few buses in Kigali, so people had to walk about on foot, tired and sweating, unaccustomed to the great elevations. They said: indeed, it is a country of a thousand hills!

Picture 3: Rwandan capital Kigali in the aftermath of the war

I have never felt such elation of the spirit, before or since. When I read today in a newspaper from some prosperous European country of how a son sues his own mother in court over property, I am stunned—I cannot imagine such a thing among my people. Truly, I am proud that I was born in Africa. In spite of the tragedy my country has had to live through, my people are in no way cruel or bad. This was impressed on me at the time the Tutsi flock came together in Rwanda in the great repatriation of 1994.

I first saw the green Rwandan hills I had heard of for so long on December 22, 1994. Indeed they were beautiful, these hills. How on earth, I wondered, could such a picture—a distilled essence of God's beauty—have been the scene, only few months before, of mass insanity?

The journey took me and my younger sister a long time because of numerous roadblocks. In the aftermath of war, soldiers of the Rwandan Patriotic Front repeatedly checked everyone's documents. Our bus arrived in Kigali at night and we could not go any further because of darkness and the curfew. Only the lights of military trucks illuminated the devastated city. Fortunately, the soldiers were friendly. They were Tutsi and they knew we were their sisters: like them we had grown up in exile, and we were now coming to our common homeland to stay. There on the front, they knew: we had always been confident of their victory. It was forbidden to move about at night, and we did not know the city; but the RPF patrol detailed a young soldier with a gun as our escort and together, well after midnight, we finally found our mother and our brother and sisters.

During those first days I remember the new feeling of seeing the whole Tutsi flock together. After so many years in Diaspora, humiliated and persecuted, we were free. We came from different countries, bringing with us our different backgrounds. Those who came from Anglophone Africa drove on the left side of the road, those from the Francophone on the right. But nearly everybody spoke good Kinyarwanda. In the streets there were endless surprise meetings of people who had known each other many years before, had been separated and now suddenly found each other again. How funny and exhilarating it was to unexpectedly meet former friends or family members; tears of joy, fond hugging and friendly exclamations were regular occurrences during those days.

It was saddening to note traces of degeneration in some of the young people. Where have they gone, I wondered, the black beauties and the great young giants of our Tutsi stock? Deprived of traditional Tutsi food, some of the young returnees did not resemble their ancestors very much. The characteristic Tutsi physical features had not disappeared, but they had clearly become less striking. And we had changed psychologically as well. Poverty and humiliation, the common companions of asylum seekers, left inevitable scars on the collective mind of my people. It was as if they could not quite believe that we were now at home, normal citizens with proper rights. It even seems to me that in many Tutsis today one thing is still missing: that unique self-esteem, self-respect and the special Tutsi imperturbability for which our people were always so rightly admired by foreigners.

Soon the government ministries opened their doors. The RPF units were turned into the regular troops of the national army. Not without difficulty, the new government started to seek a way to govern the devastated and deeply injured country. A large part of the state work force was made up of Hutus who had worked there prior to the genocide. They cautiously watched to see how the new inexperienced authorities would begin—and to see whether these authorities would seek revenge.

There was no revenge. Former active *génocidaires* were one after another identified and put in jail, where they were dressed in pink costumes of prison shirts and Bermuda shorts; but that was all. I do not remember a single episode of ethnic hostility in the streets. It was almost unbelievable to observe: the society functioned as if these two ethnicities had not passed through an unspeakably terrifying experience, as if there had not been thirty-five years of ethnic segregation.

Life started to become normal, with a daily routine. People started to look for jobs; everybody left home early in the morning to circulate from one NGO (non-governmental organization) to another. In those days, humanitarian organizations sustained many thousands of lives and provided funds which allowed the nation to resurrect itself. Classmates shared the names and addresses of potential employers and jobs, and advised one another on where one's best chances might lie. I remember the special feeling I had two weeks after coming to Kigali. I applied for a decent job; for the first time in my life I was not considered a second-rank candidate—and I was hired. This country was mine. And it needed me!

In April of 1995 the University of Rwanda, although still in ruins, had reopened. I decided to continue my studies. The National University opened its doors to all Rwandans who wished to continue their education, Hutu and Tutsi alike. During that first post-war year, some students came from abroad; others had been studying there before the war. At the university I met students and lecturers who came from many different countries. It was a great mixture of different languages and accents. Everyone brought with him a part of his past and the flavor of his background. The majority of students spoke both French and English, though some only the latter. Sometimes this created problems because there were not enough lecturers capable of teaching courses in both languages. The government started to invite lecturers from abroad.

It is hard to describe all the difficulties of the first post-war year at the university campus. Human kindness and solidarity were strikingly evident again, literally helping us to survive. Hutu and Tutsi students lived in the same compounds and shared the same buildings. As it always was in our country, with very few exceptions, everybody knows everybody else's background. Usually Tutsi students avoided sharing a room with Hutus. Otherwise there was no segregation, and no one dared to comment openly about ethnic distinctions. For me there was a special memory to deal with: I could not forget the first days of the ethnic war in Burundi. Even now I remember how students had attempted to kill their fellow students of a different ethnicity in the very midst of the university campus of Bujumbura.

Looking at us from the outside, no one could tell there was ethnic tension among the students at the National University of Rwanda. Yet an invisible wall always stood between us, keeping us from forming close relationships with students from a different ethnicity. But that was all. I do not remember any acts of violence or revenge, not even verbal abuse. When we young Tutsis were in exile, our principal frame of mind had been that we would return to Rwanda one day; we were prepared for this. Our parents taught us to think of struggle, not of revenge. It seems to me that taking a machete and killing a neighbor's child requires an overwhelming inferiority complex—which no Tutsi has. What we felt after coming to this country, now finally ours, can be described as excitement. We were both elated and yet still reluctant to believe that this had truly happened. The aftermath of the tragedy was still to be seen everywhere, of course, and thus our joy was always mixed with both grief and fear. It would not be too great an exaggeration to say that everyone still fears everyone else in our country. To deny this would be to foster a lie.

> Today, Rwandans face numerous challenges, made all the more demanding by real tests of conscience. From injured memory they must move to the search for reconciliation; avoiding the escapism of "spiritual experiences", they have to discover themselves and their future. They also have to discover Europeans, who brought Christianity to them, and who fled at the onset of genocide ten years ago.
> *The Rev. Elisée Musemakweli*

In 1996, while still at the University, I once saw some refugee Hutus who had fled the country at the end of the genocide and were now coming back. The Rwandan government had made huge efforts to convince them to return. The ones I saw must have come from the camps in the Congo: I saw them on the Gikongoro Road. There were quite a few of them, dressed in old and dirty clothes, dead tired. They were stepping down onto Rwandan soil from United Nations trucks and from big rented buses—men, women, the elderly, children, all together. Among them there must have been not only peasants, but also former intellectuals, university lecturers, businesspersons... Not all of them had participated in the genocide, but some surely had. Strangely, I felt no hate— I who lost so many members of my family. I simply saw them as refugees, which was what I had been for most of my life. I cannot forget the look in their eyes as they returned. I could see there was a struggle going on there between the fear of being killed and the impossibility of staying any longer in the camps abroad. I recognized the look of refugees. And I could not feel anything other than pity for them. How many hundreds of thousands of them are still hiding in the dense forests of the eastern Congo? How many have now found refuge across Africa, Europe and USA?

May Almighty God help my torn country. May there be no more refugees. May all of us, Tutsis and Hutus, learn to live together and to share the beauty of our common home.

Chapter 11

What Next?

Ukuri guca muziko ntigushya (The truth passes through the fire but does not burn down).
Rwandan proverb

So a historical injustice was to some extent righted: the entire Rwandan Tutsi people saw their rights restored. Tutsis are now regular citizens of Rwanda and do not feel different from anybody else. But only a very few of today's Rwandan Tutsis are actual survivors of the genocide. The great majority are either former refugees, or refugees' children who came to Rwanda as their historic homeland.

Picture 4: Kigali today

One must now ask what should come next. Perhaps, some may say, it is now the Tutsi's turn to discriminate against the

Hutu on ethnic grounds. Anyone who thinks this way does not understand the situation in today's Rwanda at all. First, Tutsis are still a clear and obvious minority in Rwanda. In all official institutions, the number of Hutus matches their percentage of the population, which continues well above ours. But beyond that, each of Tutsis knows from his or her own experience what ethnic discrimination feels like on the receiving end. It was so ugly that I, for example, can hardly imagine doing the same to other people.

The genocide has changed the demography of our provinces. In practical terms, there are now many mono-ethnic rural areas in Rwanda where Tutsi still do not live. We simply avoid going there, unless ready to face the danger. Of course, the government and the military have full control over the entire territory. But if you go there on your own…you are not safe. For example, I would think twice before taking a bus to visit our patrimony up-country. Such is the reality of today's Rwanda.

Another reality one must face is that quite a long history of exile, persecution and separation has to have an impact on any ethnicity. Anglophone Tutsis who came from Uganda still feel estranged from the Francophone Tutsis from Burundi and the Congo; each group tends to stay within its own confines. Some Tutsis even use derisive nicknames for the members of other groups. Sometimes I wonder whether we Tutsis have already forgotten our life in exile. Do all of us understand that our very survival may still be in danger? While the Tutsis make up only a tiny fraction of the population of today's Rwanda, there are no longer Tutsi diasporas in neighboring countries to draw on. I hope no Tutsi will ever lose sight of this fact:

Habgirwa benshi hakunva benebyo
(Many listen but only those concerned understand.)
Rwandan proverb

Those who once dreamed of the Final Solution are alive. They are just across the border, in the dense forests of the eastern Congo. They have kept their arms and can easily find new supplies of ammunition. Do you know the message these extremists send to Hutu youngsters? "Be fruitful, multiply, raise more Hutus! One day we will return to power!" Such sentiments can be easily found on the Internet, merely by running a search on the word "Rwanda". What turns up are predominantly Hutu extremist sites.

Hearings of the International Criminal Tribunal for Rwanda have been going on in Arusha, Tanzania, for ten years now. Only a handful of criminals have been sentenced so far. Observers say that Rwandans are unwilling to testify. This is true. It is often the case that there are no more survivors, or that those few who survived are afraid of being killed by those against whom they should testify (or their clandestine supporters). There is no safety in Rwanda for the surviving Tutsis.

> A Jewish child gassed or a Tutsi child slaughtered are killed because they were born Jewish or Tutsi. This identity disqualifies them from belonging to humanity in the eyes of their executioners. Consequently, all of humanity is called upon to claim justice on their behalf.
> *Robert Badinter*: International Criminal Tribunal Reports

One day I saw a demonstration on television. The demonstrators' placards read: "Stop Seal Hunting in Newfoundland!" and "The Seals Are Nearing Extinction!" But my people are in exactly the same situation: the hunt for innocent Tutsis is far from over; and the hunters are ready! If anyone doubts this, the reports of news services are there to be checked. In a recent issue of *The Economist* one finds:

> Before the massacre, anonymous leaflets were circulated calling for Tutsis to be killed. Then, on the night of August 13th, 2004, armed marauders overran the Gatumba camp. With guns and machetes, they shot and chopped 160 defenseless refugees to death... Small wonder that outsiders find central Africa's wars confusing.

It is not yet clear who carried out the pogrom. A Burundian rebel group claimed responsibility, but witnesses reported that Rwandan and Congolese gunmen also took part. The only certainty is that the victims were mostly Congolese Tutsis.
The Economist, August 2004

I have not seen protestors approaching their governments on the subject of the continuing extermination of the Tutsis. Indeed, **outsiders find central Africa's wars confusing**...

Every Tutsi must ask himself what to do now. I am not in position to speak for all. Nevertheless, I still have to say what I think, as all of us should:

We have to understand that none of us Rwandans can live without seeing our green hills. This is true for all of us, Hutus as well as Tutsis. As long as a Rwandan remains alive, he will long to return to his beautiful country. Rwanda has to accept its prodigal sons. They should have a way to come back to their hills.

No matter how much we like or dislike our neighbors, neither Hutus nor Tutsis can live without the other. Tutsis alone could never sustain the country's economy. Neither can the Hutus alone, as thirty years of their hard-line regime clearly demonstrated. During these thirty years, the Hutu nationalists tried to rid Rwandan life of all Tutsi participation; they were not able to do this, even with considerable foreign aid behind them. Having often accused Tutsis of aspirations for hegemony, the Hutu themselves have proven that, in the end, without the Tutsis there was a marked reversal in the country's progress. Why not use the Tutsi potential that historically belongs to this country, for the development instead of wasting such a national resource? No one from either ethnicity should have privileges; let each show his abilities for the greater good of Rwanda. Let us compete rather than fight.

Unfortunately, Rwanda has quite an ugly image all over the world. As far as the rest of humanity is concerned, there is hardly any difference between Hutu and Tutsi. Many people in the wider world still consider our nation an assembly of murderers and butchers. It will take time to persuade international public opinion that Rwandans are no different from people elsewhere. There is an ancient proverb: "A man comes into the world covered in blood; and so he leaves it." Shall we one day prove the falsehood of this proverb? Do we really bring forth our children only to see them die one day covered in blood? Rwanda needs its children alive—all of them!

We do not like to publicly pronounce the names Tutsi and Hutu. We are afraid to give additional leverage to those who purposely want to divide our nation. But the fact that we do not mention something aloud does not mean that this something has ceased to exist. Every child in Rwanda knows that the ethnicities of Hutu and Tutsi exist. And every one of us knows exactly who he or she is. What can we do about this? I think the only approach that makes sense is to discuss the matter openly—which is what I have done here. The truth cannot create divisions among people. On the contrary—it is lies that divide.

> *Uvuga ibigoramye imihoro ikarakara.*
> (Start speaking about the crooked and it is the sickle that becomes angry).
> *Rwandan proverb*

So, after all this, what to do? For good or ill, there is only one small country for all us Rwandans. Some have thought partitioning it to create a Tutsi and a Hutu land; but who should perform this partition, and how? Should we use the historical cadastral records? Or perhaps use the actual proportions of the population, now "corrected" by the bloody machetes of the *génocidaires*? These questions have no answers; and in the meantime we have to live. So instead of waiting for some theoretical resolution, let us learn how to share the land of Rwanda now— as it is.

107

Afterword

It has become evident that the Tutsis will not disappear from the face of the earth. Over and over again we produce young men who one day turn into mighty warriors and strong leaders. We do not know how we do this. Otherwise we are like everyone else. Like everyone, we do not hasten to reveal our secrets; like everyone, we are at times exceedingly proud — and sometimes pretend to be what we are not. But all this lies within the natural variations among human beings. All we ask is to be taken as we are, with all our strengths and weaknesses.

At the end of this account I feel I must address the mystery of the Tutsis — or risk leaving the reader feeling unfulfilled. Everyone understands that there must be something special in a small people which succeeded in keeping its identity in spite of unparalleled historical challenges.

This mystery is simple: we Tutsi never sleep. Like our ancestors — who spent their nights among grazing cows, ready at any moment to defend themselves and their livestock against a stealthy enemy — we never truly sleep. Among the multitude of peoples inhabiting the globe, we are the ones whose natural right to live is questioned. If a species of animal were about to disappear, and if the animals themselves could perceive this, they would probably feel the same way we do. We are ready to face death at any moment — awakening in the morning and going to bed at night; going to school and to the university; marrying and raising our children.

This eternal vigilance, this permanent Red Level of danger makes our people strong and invincible. We must survive, and we shall. If Tutsi harbor a mystery at all, this is it.

Foreigners

You may have heard of the atrocities in Rwanda before, but never thought of them as any of your business. Indeed, what on earth could you have in common with those Africans, killing each other for no apparent reason? Now you know the story of my people, the Tutsi minority—struggling for survival, suffering unspeakable losses, facing the danger of extinction.

The atrocities in Rwanda which you heard about were committed against us. Can you still claim that this is none of your business? We are humans like everyone else, and we ask no privileges but one: the privilege of living on. We do not want revenge, but life. As Rwandans, we want to live in the only place on earth we truly love— Rwanda. We will gladly make peace with our Hutu neighbors. But we warn anyone who still thinks of a return to genocide: we shall not rest while such thoughts are allowed to flourish. Though we are not many, the world would be well served to listen to us.

Rwandans

Let us first think of our children and then of ourselves. Let us agree that no one among us is more worthy to live than another. Both Hutus and Tutsis are intelligent, and enmity between us will not end in victory for one over the other. On each side we have many talented men and women; putting their skills together could greatly change our beautiful country. We can turn our small Rwanda into a modern developed nation, an exceptional country that every Rwandan will be proud of. In this country there will be no despairing cries and no blood, but a land where milk and honey pour forth on all men and women, people educated and free of prejudice. Let us amaze the entire world by creating such a nation. With God's help we can. And it is time to start:

> In spite of difficulties and frustrations of the moment, I still have a dream…
> *Martin Luther King*

Courage, Rwandans!

BIBLIOGRAPHY

Patrick de Saint-Exupéry, *L'inavouable. La France au Rwanda*, Paris, 2004.

The "Jews" of Africa, *The Economist*, Aug 21 – 27, 2004, v. 372, Number 8389.

Romeo Dallaire, L-Gen., *Shake Hands with the Devil. The Failure of Humanity in Rwanda*, Random House Canada, 2003.

Bernard Lugan, *Histoire du Rwanda: de la préhistoire à nos jours*, Paris, Bartillat, 1997.

Luc de Heusch, "Tutsis, Hutus face à l'histoire", *République* No 24, October-November 1994.

Alexis Kagame, *Un abrégé de l'Histoire du Rwanda de 1853 à 1972*, v.2, Editions Universitaires du Rwanda, Butare, 1975.

Martin Luther King Jr, "I Have a Dream. The Speech in Washington D.C. on August 28, 1963." *The Peaceful Warrior*, New York, 1968.

Antoine de Saint-Exupéry, *Terre des hommes* (first published in 1939), Paris, Gallimard, 1991.

Henry M. Stanley, *A travers le continent mystérieux*, Paris, 1879.

Henry M. Stanley, *How I Found Livingstone*, London, 1872.

Yahoo Actualité lundi le 7 juin 2004
La boîte noire de l'ONU
http://radio-canada.ca/nouvelles/International/nouvelles/2004 06/07/006-RWANDABOITENOIRE.shtml

Robert Badinter
La cour pénale internationale
http://rwandap.free.fr/comprendre.htm

Jeannine Burk
Simply Because We Were Jews
http://www.holocaustsurvivors.org/cgi-bin/data.show.pl?di=
record&da=recordings&ke=23

CERIN (Centre de recherche et d'information nutritionnelles)
Rapport No 12, février 2001
http://www.cerin.org/periodiques/AlimPreca/AlimPreca12.asp

Jean-Luc Chavanieux
En quoi le massacre des Tutsis du Rwanda est bien un génocide
http://rwanda.free.fr/docs1_b.htm

Jean Pierre Chrétien
Auditions de la Mission d'information parlementaire française sur le Rwanda, 7 avril 1998
http://www.reseauvoltaire.net/imprimer7842.html

Henry Van Dyke
Life, work, happiness
http://www.sunriseonline.ca/kings_ehighway/quotes.html

Raul Hilberg
The Aryanization of Businesses and the Night of Broken Glass
http://www.candles-museum.com/holocaus.htm

Thierry Leftmaster
Notre honte à tous
http://www.tou-o.com/article.php?lire=54

Elisée Musemakweli
Radio Swiss Romande: en direct de la paroisse presbytérienne
de Kiyovu à Kigali
http://events.rsr.ch/rwanda/archives/2004/04/18

Jacques Seebacher
Ce que c'est que l'exil: Colloque international sur l'exil et la
tolérance, Paris, 15 novembre 2002
http://www.senat.fr/evenement/colloque_vhugo.html

Claudine Vidal
Audition de la mission d'information parlementaire française
sur le Rwanda le 24 mars 1998
http://www.reseauvoltaire.net/imprimer7838.html

Simon Wiesenthal Center
Museum of Tolerance
http://motlc.wiesenthal.com/resources/questions/

INDEX

Mwami, 53, 54

N

National Guard troops, 57
National School Competition Test, 68
National Socialist-style fascism, 10
Nazis, 9, 60, 79, 90
Nazism in Europe, 65
New York City, 83
Night of Broken Glass, 65, 111
Non-Rwandans, 9

O

Oceania, 19
Oscar Baumann, 39

P

Paul Kagame, 72
Presbyterian, 33, 45, 71, 77, 88
Presbyterian Church, 45, 88
President Habyarimana, 71, 74
President Obote, 70
Presidential cortège, 75
Pygmies, 15, 25

R

Red Level, 108
Rift Valley, 17
Robespierre, 51
RPF, 72, 73, 88, 92, 93, 97, 98
Ruanda-Urundi, 15, 37
Rwanda, 7, 8, 9, 10, 15, 17, 18, 19, 20, 21, 23, 25, 28, 31, 32, 33, 34, 35, 36, 38, 39, 40, 41, 43, 44, 45, 47, 48, 51, 52, 53, 54, 55, 56, 58, 59, 60, 61, 63,
64, 65, 66, 68, 71, 72, 73, 75, 76, 77, 79, 80, 81, 82, 83, 85, 87, 89, 91, 92, 93, 95, 97, 99, 100, 103, 104, 105, 106, 107, 108, 109, 110, 111, 112
Rwandan anthropologists, 60
Rwandan genocide, 9, 79, 82
Rwandan hills, 8, 77, 97
Rwandan landscape, 45
Rwandan Patriotic Front, 72, 77, 87, 88, 93, 97
Rwandan Tutsis, i, iii, 8, 15, 60, 63, 68, 76, 82, 95, 103
Rwandans, 10, 14, 15, 18, 19, 28, 31, 32, 36, 40, 44, 48, 54, 66, 70, 74, 81, 82, 93, 99, 100, 105, 106, 107, 109
Ryangombe, 45

S

Scotsman, 14
Scottish propaganda, 52
shocking photographs, 9
Socialists, 48
Sporadic killings, 59
St. Bartholomew's Night, 79
Swahili caravan, 38

T

Tanzania, 17, 36, 73, 105
the Kanzenze Bridge, 57
Tibetan, 59
Trusteeship, 53
Turks, 79
Tutsi, i, iii, iv, 7, 8, 9, 10, 13, 15, 16, 17, 18, 19, 21, 22, 23, 24, 25, 26, 27, 29, 32, 33, 34, 36, 37, 39, 40, 41, 45, 47, 48, 52, 53, 54, 56, 57, 58, 59, 60, 61, 64, 65, 66, 67, 69, 70, 71, 73, 74, 75, 77, 79, 80, 81, 83, 85,

86, 87, 88, 89, 90, 91, 92, 95,
97, 98, 99, 100, 103, 104, 105,
106, 107, 108, 109
Tutsi aristocrat, 29
Tutsi potential, 106
Tutsis, 8, 11, 15, 19, 21, 25, 26,
27, 31, 36, 38, 48, 49, 52, 54,
55, 57, 58, 59, 60, 61, 63, 64,
66, 67, 68, 70, 71, 72, 73, 74,
75, 76, 77, 81, 84, 85, 86, 87,
88, 90, 91, 92, 93, 94, 95, 98,
100, 101, 103, 104, 105, 106,
108, 109, 110, 111
Twa, 15, 16, 19, 21, 22, 23, 25,
59, 64

U

Uganda, 17, 38, 63, 64, 70, 72,
104

UN High Commission for
Refugees, 70
urugo, 30, 31, 33, 34, 61

V

Virgin Mary, 56
vitamins, 26
von Götzen, 40

W

Western world, 10

Z

Zanzibar, 38

Ordering this book and other books by Adonis & Abbey Publishers

Wholesale inquiries in the UK and Europe:
Gardners Books Ltd
+44 1323 521777: email: custcare@gardners.com

Wholesale enquiries in USA and Canada
Ingram Book Company (ordering)
+1 800 937 8000 website: www.ingrambookgroup.com

*Online Retail Distribution: All leading online book sellers
including www.amazon.co.uk, www.amazon.com,
www.barnesandnoble.com

*Shop Retail: Ask any good bookshop or contact our office:
http//:www.Adonis-abbey.com

Phone: +44 (0) 207 793 8893

www.ingramcontent.com/pod-product-compliance
Lightning Source LLC
Chambersburg PA
CBHW032105080426
42733CB00006B/426